Reflections on practice

Series editor: Richard Johnstone

Language teaching in the mirror

Edited by Antony Peck
and David Westgate

CiLT

REFLECTIONS ON PRACTICE

Editorial Committee
Professor Richard Johnstone, University of Stirling
Professor Chris Brumfit, University of Southampton
Dr Michael Byram, University of Durham
Ute Hitchin, CILT
Dr Lid King, CILT
Paul Meara, University College of Swansea
Dr Rosamond Mitchell, University of Southampton
Antony Peck, University of York
David Westgate, University of Newcastle-upon-Tyne

First published 1994
Copyright © 1994 Centre for Information on Language Teaching and Research
ISBN 1 874016 22 4

Cover by Logos Design and Advertising
Printed in Great Britain by Bell & Bain Ltd

Published by the Centre for Information on Language Teaching and Research, 20 Bedfordbury, Covent Garden, London WC2N 4LB.

Contents

Preface

In recent years the teaching and learning of languages has assumed unprecedented importance throughout the world and has led to an enormous number of publications. Many of these contain practical material written by various groups for teachers, while others are written by researchers for researchers.

CILT's new series REFLECTIONS ON PRACTICE breaks new ground by linking these two very different worlds. It consists of material written mainly by teachers but within the framework of classroom-based action research, and supported through collaboration with experienced researchers - in this first case, Antony Peck and David Westgate who are both already well known for their work in classrooms. It becomes evident that this form of collaboration is to the clear mutual benefit of each party and has considerable potential for supporting the new forms of pre-service teacher education and continuing professional development of teachers that are coming into place.

The first title in the series, *Language teaching in the mirror*, introduces the concept of the reflective practitioner of language teaching and serves as a foundation for the series as a whole. Each subsequent title will develop the notion of reflection on practice in relation to a specific domain, beginning with modern foreign languages at primary school.

Professor Richard Johnstone
Series editor: REFLECTIONS ON PRACTICE

Chapter 1

Why reflect on practice?

'Reflection on practice' can mean different things to different teachers. To begin with, all would claim to engage in reflection on teaching in the sense of at least brief and informal planning and review of lessons. All the same, the first idea which the term 'reflection on practice' may bring to mind is more akin to research, something done from outside or after the events in which teachers themselves are involved, and carried out mostly by specialists and sometimes by (superhuman!) teacher-researchers.

This book challenges such assumptions and seeks to provide means by which teachers, including languages teachers, can integrate some systematic reflection in a more down-to-earth, matter-of-fact way into their work. It offers a perspective in which teachers come to take it as read that aspects of what they do merit their professional curiosity and that they have the capacity, as professionals, to gather and take account of some relevant evidence. This book is predominantly written by teachers who report and share reflections on a wide range of topics. The latter embrace e.g. basic concerns of a newly qualified teacher, selected everyday aspects of teaching behaviour or pupil response, as well as issues requiring longer-term investigation for which particular teachers may be especially well-placed. What unites the contributors is their commitment to being reflective.

Constraints

It has of course to be acknowledged that teaching often takes place too quickly and too intuitively for teachers to be able to reflect in any systematic way about what they are doing or have just done. Classroom life is frequently too hectic, which is why any time which can be ear-marked for reflection is highly valued. It is also true that the pressure against reflection which is the rule for most teachers applies with special force to teachers of modern foreign languages (MFL). Various studies have stressed the demanding lead-role played by MFL teachers (e.g. Peck, 1988; Mitchell et al, 1981), particularly in the presentation and consolidation of new language through routines of teacher-focused, class-based, oral work. Like most teachers, MFL practitioners conduct their classes in such a way as to 'tell pupils when to talk, what to talk about, when to stop talking and how well they talked', at least for much of the time. MFL teachers, however, can 'appear also to prescribe the very words, even features of words, with which to talk' (Westgate et al, 1985; p276). While it is true that a lot of ingenuity has recently gone into devising strategies for passing more of the communicative initiative from teachers to pupils (Peck, 1990), many MFL classrooms are still places where second-by-second managerial demands of an especially heavy and subtle kind are made upon the teacher, with inhibiting consequences for reflection.

The general dependency of MFL teachers upon 'methodological' advice from outside their classrooms, of which there has been no shortage in recent decades (Phillips, 1988), has been very understandable. Since implementation of the National Curriculum orders (September 1992) external pressures upon MFL teachers have further increased. In all probability they will not abate until substantial familiarity with planning, 'delivery' and assessment has been gained with all the year groups concerned.

Extending good practice

Fortunately, however, many are able to see the 'new' ways of working as extensions or adaptations of practice developed in anticipation (see the contributions to this or later chapters by e.g. John Batey, Diana Kent, Jacky Ramage and Margaret Wells). Much of what is now being officially advocated also represents an intention to disseminate widely within the profession what reports have called the good practice observed in individual classrooms around the country (e.g. DES/Welsh Office, 1990; Chapter 10). It is in no way to denigrate those good practices, many of which have themselves resulted from highly systematic kinds of reflection, nevertheless to observe that a policy of attempting to transplant them from their original contexts to a range of quite different ones may give rise to problems. Indeed it is the very nature of those problems which lie at the heart of the answer to the question with which this chapter began: 'Why reflect upon practice?'.

By the argument presented so far, a short answer might be: 'to be truly professional'. Nearly all jobs rely on a body of accumulated experience; many also draw upon an established body of knowledge about procedures, effects and contexts. Those claiming to be professions typically require individual practitioners not only to possess such knowledge but to display judgement in using it. That means more than following instructions; it means interpreting knowledge in the light of particular circumstances, appropriately and to best effect. Applying such a definition of professional behaviour to teaching puts curriculum delivery in a fresh light. It reminds us that teacher effectiveness (no less) depends to a considerable extent upon teachers' knowledge of the contexts in which they operate, including their own and their pupils' relevant characteristics, and upon their skill at devising materials and activities which will work. Behind such skill lies reflection - which, to be fully productive, involves some systematic experimentation and evaluation, the results of which get fed back into teaching and, when appropriate, more widely shared.

This point of view is explained and expanded in a general way by the first contributor to this chapter.

Here Chris Kyriacou, a former comprehensive school teacher of maths, and subsequently a researcher experienced in promoting teachers' reflection, defines 'reflective practice' more closely, gives chapter and verse for the origins of the idea, and sets an agenda of questions which are followed up throughout the book.

REFLECTIVE TEACHING IN A WIDER CONTEXT
by Chris Kyriacou

All teachers think about their teaching. Indeed, it is difficult to conceive how it would be possible to teach without continually monitoring and reflecting on one's practice. However, since the early 1980s, increasing attention has been paid by educational researchers to the notion of 'reflective teaching'. In essence, reflective teaching refers to an approach to teaching in which teachers regularly think about and evaluate their own practice in a systematic way with a view to developing and further improving their classroom practice. Whilst it has already been recognised that all teachers think about their teaching, it is still possible for teachers to adopt an uncritical and mechanistic approach to their teaching for much of the time. Reflective teaching goes beyond simply thinking about one's teaching on an occasional basis. Rather it refers to an orientation towards one's own practice which is based on inquiry and problem solving. It refers to a stance in which teachers positively seek to explore their current practice.

Reflection-in-action

One of the most important writings in this area was that of Donald Schön (1983). Schön looked at how professionals in a variety of occupations reflected on their current practice. He referred to these as 'reflective practitioners'. As a result of his analysis, Schön made an important distinction between 'reflection-in-action' and 'reflection-on-action'. Reflection-in-action refers to teachers reflecting on their classroom practice whilst actually engaged in the lesson itself, thereby coming to see a classroom situation or activity in a new light. Reflection-on-action refers to teachers reflecting on their teaching after the lesson has finished. Reflection-on-action is deliberate and systematic, and may occur in the staffroom during a coffee break, or perhaps much later when reviewing students' progress. Whilst both reflection-in-action and reflection-on-action are important, Schön argued that it is the reflective practitioners' ability constantly to frame and reframe a problem during reflection-in-action, in particular, that lies at the heart of the expertise held by experienced professionals.

Essential characteristics

The notion of reflective teaching, however, is not a new one. Pollard and Tann (1987) identify four essential characteristics. These are that reflective teaching:

- implies an active concern with aims and consequences, as well as with means and technical efficiency;

- combines inquiry and implementation skills with attitudes of open-mindedness, responsibility and wholeheartedness;

- is applied in a cyclical or spiralling process, in which teachers continually monitor, evaluate and revise their own practice;

- is based on teacher judgement, informed partly by self-reflection and partly by insights from educational disciplines.

The growth of interest in reflective teaching stems in great measure from the increased recognition that, to a large extent, teachers are and will always be the main agents of their own professional growth. Those teachers who regularly think about their teaching are much more likely to continue to develop and improve their classroom practice. As a result, a number of initial teacher training courses and in-service training (INSET) courses have developed with the explicit intention to promote student teachers' or experienced teachers' ability to reflect on their own practice regularly and effectively.

Reflective teaching: pre-service

In the case of student teachers, this has typically involved such activities as requiring them to conduct a written review of particular lessons on a regular basis, carrying out and evaluating a particular classroom teaching activity, and keeping a diary or profile of their own thinking and progress. Such activities are designed to build up a reflective attitude towards teaching and to introduce methods to help with such reflection. It is argued that initial teacher training cannot possibly produce teachers who know all they need to know about classroom practice and, as such, it is vital that student teachers are helped to adopt an approach to thinking about their teaching which will provide a basis for further development (see Tabachnick and Zeichner, 1991).

Reflective teaching: in-service

In the case of experienced teachers, INSET courses designed to encourage reflective teaching have typically required the teacher to monitor and evaluate some aspect of their current classroom practice and to introduce and evaluate some type of change to their current classroom practice. This often involves data collection such as audio taping a lesson, collecting feedback from pupils, or making use of a colleague acting as a classroom observer (see Calderhead and Gates, 1993; Kyriacou, 1991; Russell and Munby, 1992). A number of researchers have found that the opportunity to share their problems and insights with other experienced teachers who were also engaged in monitoring and evaluating their own practice was particularly effective, and this is now a feature of many such INSET courses. In addition to INSET courses, a number of self-development packs for school and staff development have been produced which include activities designed to promote reflection on current practice. For example, Smith's (1990) pack on classroom practice includes such activities as comparing views on effective and ineffective teaching styles, the use of an observation schedule by a trusted colleague that can help focus attention on key features of a lesson, and descriptions of classroom situations to which teachers are asked to consider their responses. Such activities are very useful in helping teachers to reflect on a variety of aspects of their current practice, and by doing so with colleagues can help promote whole-school approaches and greater consistency between staff.

Finally, writings about reflective teaching have raised a host of important questions that need to be addressed.

- WHAT SHOULD BE REFLECTED UPON?
  Clearly, almost everything a teacher does is complex. How should a teacher best decide what is worth reflecting on? Should it simply rely on teachers' personal agendas or their response to personal concerns, or should this decision be influenced by others?

- HOW SHOULD THE REFLECTION BE CONDUCTED?
  Is it sufficient simply to explore one's ideas on an ad hoc basis or talk to pupils and colleagues, or should the reflection be more systematic, rigorous and research-oriented?

- WHAT IMPLICATIONS DOES THE PROCESS OF REFLECTION HAVE?
  Does it have implications for the teacher, for other teachers, for pupils, and for the school? Are there ethical issues involved? Is it fair and proper to be

'trying things out' with pupils without consulting them or others? Does reflective teaching place demands on others?

- HOW CAN REFLECTIVE TEACHING BEST BE ENCOURAGED?
  Some teachers seem to be more disposed towards reflective teaching than others, and some teachers seem to learn more from reflective teaching than others. It is also more likely to be adopted and to be successful within some school organisations (such as those where there is an ethos of critical discussion and change) than others. What can and should teachers, schools and others do to promote a climate within which reflective teaching is encouraged and is successful? Are there teachers for whom encouragement towards reflective teaching may be counterproductive?

Whilst interest in reflective teaching is continuing to increase, it is extremely important to build up a broader understanding of how and when it can be used to best effect. A number of case studies by teachers, outlining their own experience of reflective teaching, are beginning to provide some insights regarding its effective use. There is still, however, a great need for more such experiences to be disseminated and discussed if the issues involved in reflective teaching are to be adequately addressed and understood and thereby form a basis for the development of good practice.

Two examples now follow the kind of case studies referred to by Chris Kyriacou. Both contributors are heads of MFL departments in 13-18 high schools and both describe projects which involve collaboration with their colleagues. The two teachers differ in their starting points and, to some extent, in their goals. The first, John Batey, was drawn into processes of reflection, together with some of his colleagues, through his positive response to an approach made from his local university department of education (UDE). The second, Margaret Wells, was quite independently attracted by the idea of a longitudinal study of the way pupils responded to different types of MFL grammar teaching over time; also by the challenge of study at PhD level.

John Batey here describes a project of collaborative reflection which has now lasted a decade, but which has had two main periods of more intensive and systematic exploration. The starting point was David Westgate's idea of combining renewed contact with the classroom in a teaching role with setting up a classroom-based research study which would work 'from the inside out'. John Batey was the head of department who said 'yes'. This account locates justifications for the project within its modes of work, its outcomes and a multiplicity of associated benefits. John does not always approach reflection prosaically...

In the autumn of nineteen eighty three
A letter arrived from our lecturer friend
Revealing how he hoped he could see
A way to help him buck the trend
And welcome a trainer back to school
To the classroom no less, to use the tools
Of the trade whose skills were abundant
But needed experience recent and relevant.

A teacher trainer eager to teach
Was a beast so rare we searched for motives
Wondered whether he would come to preach
To the drifting pedagogic natives.
Indeed he talked of interaction
In the language class when the true reaction
Of sterner colleagues to noise and talk
Was to bemoan the demise of board and chalk.

However, teach he did within our team
To the surprise of many, including himself,
Once the pace of life outside academe
Blew the dust away from his library shelf.
In classes shared and lessons taught
His gentle manner and careful thought
Drew puzzled joy from pupils, normally prudent,
Isn't he rather old for a student?

The pace of our life, though frantic at best
And controlled, though I use the word loosely,
By bells, left so little time for pausing at rest
To consider the questions swirling profusely
But posed in the calm of long post-school sessions
To reveal a surprise - what was missing was tension.
Our new teacher had changed in the hours we'd spend
From lecturer-colleague to critical friend.

Continuing collaboration
by John Batey

Enough of whimsy. As was said on the occasion of our first shared publication: 'We've been speaking prose all along!'. So shall we continue.

When David Westgate approached us with an invitation to share in a practical study of life inside a modern language classroom, two aspects proved tempting: he talked of 'attempting to gain sufficient first-hand understanding of our classrooms as context' and 'of time for working and talking with teachers being essential; as too were the procedures of discussing recordings with teacher and pupil participants'. Here, we felt, was someone who seemed to want to begin his studies at anything but a safe distance and who certainly did not see what happened in language lessons as in a way divorced from the wider reality of social and school life. He could not be all bad who wrote of 'practical involvement, with group teaching and some whole-class teaching'. In any case, an extra teacher for a term with no payment required was an offer no-one could refuse. And since then his study has become our study, as well as ours his.

The proposed title of what we could do together, 'language interaction in modern language classrooms', was sufficiently awesome for teachers who had long been used to working at jogging pace at best, perhaps even at a run, and rarely paused to allow the thinking which underpinned their work to develop any hard clarity. This (without on reflection being fully aware of it) was to prove of major importance. It is clear with hindsight that the department was ripe for the development which our involvement in that project was to bring us. We were happy to reflect on the processes which every action in our working lives set in train; we recognised differences in our teaching but had never rationalised the degree to which our solidarity as a team gave strength to our variety.

A pattern of inquiry

The only problem we had in the early days of the collaboration was that David asked the questions as they arose - and they were mostly 'why?' questions. These covered, for instance, dealings with individual pupils, which seemed naturally enough to be guided by the implicit account taken of individual pupil histories ('Why use that boy to play the waiter?', 'Weren't you rather hard on Jenny?'); but they also embraced more technical issues, to do with changes in pace or lesson plan, or with evaluating pupils' FL responses in particular ways, which depended upon quick intuitive decisions. David soon realised that 'Can we talk about this?' had to give way to the pace and hectic routine of school life. Answers could be attempted only later.

Thus it was, though, that a pattern of inquiry developed. It had no fixed agenda at the start, a feature which we later were to realise was common to so-called 'ethnographic' inquiry, and which was a real bonus. Since details which first intrigued the visitor could be answered only by teachers and pupils, the focus of attention began simply with the teaching-learning process without pre-conception as to what might emerge. Understanding grew out of shared questions and a search for answers which were accessible only through tapping into the 'local knowledge' of the teachers and through trying to make explicit the hitherto unarticulated rationale of individual teachers' strategies and techniques. In that way our agenda got talked into existence - and has kept evolving ever since.

Blurring the boundaries

It has thus also never seemed to be reflection or research for its own sake and we have no recollection of feeling in any way threatened by the questioning, even at the start - although for instance, 'Why did you prefer to use your own material then and not the exercise in the textbook?' could put you on the spot. Perhaps it is precisely because the questioner had deliberately placed himself in a vulnerable position by taking the mantle of inexperience relative to the full-time teachers, that we very quickly found ourselves conducting a truly professional dialogue. Our roles were different, certainly, but it was from the beginning a dialogue of equals. Our second collaborative paper expresses it thus:

> Such blurring of boundaries between partners' roles does not devalue the specific contributions which each partner brings to collaborative inquiry. On the contrary, we suggest that blurred boundaries constitute a necessary condition for enhanced mutual respect. Reciprocity, in other words, maximises individual contributions and makes the whole potentially greater than the sum of its parts (Westgate et al, 1990).

We could have added with equal justification that genuine collaboration can have a significant and positive bearing on individuals' understanding as well as on more generalised outcomes.

Our work has been in two main phases, at least as far as data-gathering is concerned: Term 2 in both 1983 and 1988, with subsequent analysis and other forms of collaboration maintaining fairly continuous contact. In 1983 we decided to work with three classes and three teachers: a Year 10 German class, an upper-band Year 9 French class and a lower-band French class. In 1988, one upper-band and one lower-band class in Year 9 and one Year 10 class were involved, all for French. The school is a 13+ comprehensive high school, so Year 9 were on both occasions quite new to us. At first, David had to spend some time familiarising himself with our working patterns; and on both occasions we had to get classes used to being observed before we could launch into making - with the aid of an expert technician - a video recording of a series of lessons. Both times, too, an interview with the teacher was recorded immediately after each lesson had ended. David took responsibility over subsequent weeks for transcribing video passages and presented these for general discussion by us all.

Studies of videos and transcripts

The next step each time was for the teaching-research team to view the videos and transcripts. We did this for three reasons:

- in order to clarify details of the transcripts ('What did you think was going on just here? Why would he say that? Was that exactly what she did say?');
- to discuss some of our own actions during the lessons ('Why did you smile just then? Was it worth spending all that time on that pupil at that point?');
- to consider the teaching-learning process, i.e. more general issues. (At one stage, the idea of 'successful' pupils being ones who would 'play the game required' struck us as a useful focusing idea.)

All these activities, but particularly the second and third, have had long-lasting effects. Had we not been genuinely interested, and had a genuinely sympathetic and supportive relationship not begun to develop, the project might well have collapsed in embarrassment at this critical stage. As things were, it thrived.

Our working together since the initial collaboration has taken many forms. The climate of reflection has settled to touch all who have worked in the department, whether they were there originally or not. All have contributed in some way to the PGCE course in the UDE. We have a continuing responsibility for providing some additional teaching practice visits to PGCE students; we have represented the UDE at conferences and at deliberations about the future of initial teacher training; we have published together (see our Chapter 3 entry); we have made video recordings which have been used in several aspects of research and teaching; the 'visitor' has shared a school journey to Paris and has become a governor of the school. Most importantly, we are still friends and always accessible to each other at a time of considerable change in language teaching.

Conflicting realities

For example, the benefits of our work together are not limited to the findings about interaction within the modern language classroom, interesting and valuable as these are; they extend to what has grown from the **process** of collaborative reflection. It is beyond question that our classroom-based inquiries, and particularly the filming of lessons, has helped us to understand better the nature of the tasks facing our pupils and how pupils respond to these tasks. It became clear, for instance, that some hated 'coming out to the front', while others thrived on that and found desk work tedious. Reflecting the title of a publication to emerge from the second round of filming, we continue to be starkly aware of the conflicting 'classroom realities' of the various participants in any modern language lesson (Westgate, 1990). We have come to appreciate for how many pupils the pleasure of success within the narrow context of the classroom is at least as important as achieving officially sanctioned goals in a changing world; and how, for others, feelings about limited success are made bearable by their own ingenious survival strategies.

For us, the ever-present thorn of an open mind means that, thus far, the National Curriculum brings not constraints, but rather a drive to share collaborative development with more of our teaching colleagues. I wonder if the climate is right for another bout of study-leave.

The next account, by Margaret Wells, mostly concerns her motivation; her second contribution, in Chapter 4, focuses more on content detail.

Here she is quite explicit not only about her reasons for pushing her reflection into the realm of action research but also about her topic and the framework of a higher degree. She lists some of the benefits of which she is already conscious, but does not pull any punches when it comes to the costs, mostly in time and effort associated with the large scale of her undertaking, or to the difficulties of keeping things going.

THE LONELINESS OF THE LONG-DISTANCE REFLECTOR
by Margaret Wells

I need to reflect on my practice since I stand only five years away from retirement at age sixty and could, in fact, retire earlier. As the job itself becomes harder, the urge to reflect on long-standing concerns has intensified. My chance to do some serious reflecting in a practical way has become a 'now or never' thing. I have decided to approach it via study towards a PhD. In this form, it will occupy most or all of my remaining time until retirement, and I hope to have something in the hand when I go.

Classroom research itself embraces a substantial section of my timetabled work at school, which means that a daily amount of time is given to the project by myself and colleagues in my department, regularly, reliably and unavoidably. It also embraces a lot of what would be free time, but I will perhaps feel satisfied to retire, when the time comes, from a practice which I have already sought to boost within the last ten years through the acquisition of two masters degrees, one in my subject and the other in Education. Through these opportunities, I refreshed my knowledge and awareness of my business as a linguist and as a teacher, also I raised my state of self-confidence quite considerably. Now, the new research project and the PhD goal have become a challenge which I cannot resist.

My search for an appropriate PhD topic necessitated an examination of my modern languages practice over the past decades. The most fascinating factor was the issue of grammar teaching, central to every new teaching methodology (see further report in Chapter 4) and central also to the history of complaints and accusations which have been heaped upon practitioners in this country. My mind was more firmly made up on grammar teaching, moreover, when I looked ahead to examine the policy on which my remaining years of practice would be based. Namely, the National Curriculum Proposal for Modern Languages (final proposal, October 1990) clarified for me its position on grammar - and, importantly, the use of the target language as the conveyor of classroom methodology - in a set of provocative assumptions which provided the very challenge that I needed in order to refine my research proposal and link my past classroom practice with present practice and practice still to be shaped. I refer to the methodology argued in section 9.14 to 9.22.

Benefits of reflection

I should now like to acknowledge a variety of compensations and rewards of reflection upon practice which include the following:

- the sense of satisfaction and the self-confidence which are won through achievement;
- the benefit of enjoying sustained motivation which is reflected in all that the student does, and generates energy, vitality and dynamism;
- the ability to transcend the potentially demoralising situation facing all teachers when their pupils, regardless of age, ability and motivation, make use of only a relative amount of the teacher's input, effort and knowledge;
- the overall preservation of the teacher's state of sanity, when as researcher and student he or she enjoys a sense of fulfilment, maximises the effort put in and compensates for any disappointments encountered.

Further points could be added to this list of the psychological benefits which may be gained by the reflective teacher. Rather than cite more points, however, I would simply argue that a positive outlook is, indeed, achieved and this allows teachers to elevate themselves over and beyond the problems inherent in their task and the hard discipline of actually carrying it through. It becomes difficult in the end to know the order of cause and effect, as in the chicken and egg analogy; whether the sense of motivation helps one to transcend the difficulties and the pressures which are encountered, or whether the latter, as they occur, only serve to increase the researcher's determination to accomplish the task which fired the enthusiasm to accept its challenge in the first place. In the overall exercise, the process and the product may be of equal value and importance. In any case, the better practical understanding that I am hoping to find will make my past practice a valid, cemented reality and will illumine the practice still ahead of me.

Perhaps there will be some people who will find my investigation interesting. There will certainly be others who will make their own practice-based reflections and inquiries. It would be a very good thing, I believe, for a variety of reasons and not least for the reason of broadening the awareness of modern languages pedagogy in this country and of neutralising at least some of the criticisms levelled against it, if more classroom teachers could be encouraged to conduct research into their subject practice. Proper reflection with feedback into schools and teacher training establishments could eventually open up a more confident and successful subject arena, in which practitioners and teaching methods receive praise rather than reprimand and where teachers are seen to be as productive as those in some other much applauded European communities.

Investigating from within

We owe it to future generations of pupils, as their need to acquire competence in foreign languages increases daily, to investigate our classroom business from within, with a proper sense of purpose and a will to apply our findings to the improvement of the services which we are employed to give. It is no longer sufficient to leave the responsibility for reflection to professional researchers who borrow our classrooms as the settings for their inquiries. They do not necessarily directly offer feedback through which to influence the work that continues to go on there, and the incumbent teachers do not necessarily liaise with them, so that knowledge or information leading to improved practice may be spread. Without our taking an active role in the shaping and in the developing of the pedagogical business for which we are responsible, we surely place ourselves in the position of forever having to suffer criticism of our practice, and of continuing to have untried policies imposed upon us by external agents. I refer again to the National Curriculum Final Proposal of October 1990, containing the methodology-related assumptions already alluded to, and to the National Curriculum Final Orders for Modern Languages (1992), reflecting the same claims concerning implicit grammar teaching and target language use which by now have become the core concern of my reflection and of my PhD investigation.

'But why do a PhD? Why not simply do the inquiry exercise, the reflection for its own sake?' I feel that the exercise itself will be better for having been done in this framework. If all goes well, I shall have obtained something valuable which cannot be taken away from me. On a larger scale, I shall have been practising what I preach to my students at school, namely: 'Always leave a classroom having learned something new to take away with you'.

To be absolutely honest, as a teacher for whom retirement is imminent, I cannot imagine leaving teaching without doing something special in order to 'round off' my practice and experience, specifically, without doing the reflective exercise which I have described. The award of the PhD will tell me that I did that, that I made some sort of contribution, that, in fact, I had a place there in real terms. I cannot conceive a happier way to complete an important and long phase of one's life than to be able to consolidate the experience of it and take it away in such a tangible form.

What links these contributions might be summarised by what John Batey refers to as 'the thorn of an open mind' in relation to everyday professional practice; perhaps a 'need to reflect' (in Margaret Wells' words); certainly an awareness of benefits directly or obliquely gained. Both write of the pleasures of reflective inquiry although, as might be expected, a solo PhD student emphasises collaboration rather less and long-term goals rather more. Both explicitly value the understandings which they feel they are tentatively establishing and the consequent sense of having some hand in their own professional development. Both are prepared to say that aspects of their own practice have come under more conscious control, changed in often subtle ways. Both show sufficient self-belief to offer to share their insights or questions with others, in relation to long-standing issues.

Their contributions show clearly how 'reflection' embraces both ends of the development-research continuum. Activities at either end, and points in-between, are all legitimate, potentially rewarding and enriching. Of course, such validity does not depend upon awards or publications. Being open-mindedly reflective about one's agenda is closer to the spirit of 'reflective practice' than simply taking on a big project. The latter may nevertheless benefit from originating in modest but habitual reflection - in the cycles of review, experimentation and evaluation which can lead towards improved practice, refined objectives, new materials, clearer pictures of learning, better-understood classroom relationships... or whatever.

It is to a range of such topics that contributors direct our attention in the chapter which follows.

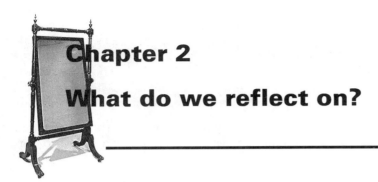

Chapter 2

What do we reflect on?

The message of this chapter is that language teaching is an enormously complex process, and that to reflect on one's own practice is itself something that has to be learned.

The first contribution, from Emma Taylor, shows a talented trainee teacher thinking about some of the many issues confronting a beginner during a period of block teaching practice. This is the central part of the Post-graduate Certificate in Education course. Emma has to cope with the challenges of being in an unfamiliar school with new colleagues, an as yet unknown school and department ethos, and a range of classes. She has to establish a relationship with several different groups of pupils, also with her new colleagues, while at the same time preparing herself to be observed by other members of staff, not to mention her university tutor! While trying to settle down in this unfamiliar social situation, she has to prepare lessons, become familiar with teaching materials in use at the school, as well as develop some of her own, and of course give the lessons she has prepared. Through her frank, direct and fresh self-evaluation, Emma gives us a rare opportunity to understand something of this complex process.

Jacky Ramage shows us how a mature teacher, at the height of her powers, is able to focus on a certain aspect of her teaching. The overall learning-teaching process is no less complex for her than it is for Emma Taylor, but for the experienced practitioner it is possible to see the details clearly enough to experiment with one or another of them. In her contribution, Jacky describes how she manipulated certain techniques of oral teaching in order to develop her pupils' fluency in speaking. Her essay has the double perspective of the experiment itself and its lasting effects some time later on in her career.

These contributions, taken together, show the all-pervading relevance of techniques of reflection to language teaching in general. The newly qualified Emma Taylor shows us the way.

REFLECTING DURING TEACHING PRACTICE
by Emma Taylor and Antony Peck

Foreign language teaching is so complex an activity, and the response of pupils so varied, that the difficulty is to choose what to reflect on, with a view to self-improvement.

There is perhaps no better way of demonstrating both the complexity of language teaching, and the need to think about it clearly, than to track the concerns of a trainee teacher on teaching practice. Every reader will recognise the thoughts and worries described here, and know them as their own. It is simply that they are expressed with a directness and freshness because they are being experienced for the first time.

Emma Taylor was a post-graduate trainee at the Language Teaching Centre of York University in 1992/93. She is a graduate of German and French. All language PGCE students at York are required to develop a set of teaching materials as an assessed item of work. These are produced during the thirteen-week block teaching practice, together with the plans for the lessons when they were used, and an on-going evaluation of the lessons, intended to give trainees practice and experience of reflecting on their own teaching.

Jotting down immediate reactions

Together with the other trainees in her group, Emma had been introduced to some techniques of reflection during the university-based part of the course, before teaching practice. However, as she subsequently said, amongst the possible techniques, the best method of reflecting, for her, had been to jot down her immediate reactions after the end of the lesson. We are fortunate that she did this, because we have a vivid account of the early stages of reflection. It has the ring of truth. Moreover, Emma's concerns are ours.

The lessons referred to here are with two different year groups. The evaluations were written on lesson plans handed in with her set of teaching materials. The lessons were delivered in a comprehensive school in the north of England and span the period 14 January to 25 February 1993.

It is not always quite clear what precise aspect of the lesson Emma is referring to, but this is because she is writing for herself, at the end of a lesson. Unlike Cecily's diary, these evaluations were not intended for publication! The quality of the reflection, however, is abundantly apparent.

The first four evaluations come from lessons given to Year 13.

The first one shows Emma thinking about students' reaction to her, the difficulties of getting them to speak, how to implement her plan and how to pitch the lesson accurately.

> ### *Evaluation*
>
> Initial part of lesson was a little stilted. VI formers tend to be a little apprehensive of seeing a new face. Slight inhibitions/shyness/ reluctance to speak. Second part of lesson ran quite smoothly (as my confidence also improved). There are five in the class. Two girls - very conscientious. Two boys - not so academic - they also seemed a little baffled by the nature of the text. Next week I shall have to use a simpler text. Also, need more 'motivating' texts to get the students to speak.

Here, we find her reflecting on the difficulties of motivating students, even those in Year 13, also on how to get through the work she wanted to do, and how to elicit responses.

> ### *Evaluation*
>
> The class this morning was very average. I found it very difficult to motivate the group. They spent most of the lesson yawning and playing with their hair. The work was covered, however, and in as much detail as feasibly possible. I found myself asking questions, however, and then, being faced with a deadly silence, I had to answer most of my own questions!

Success! The rewards!

> ### *Evaluation*
>
> The reading comprehension seems to have been good practice for the students. Under pressure, students were able to elicit answers very quickly. The role-play worked very well. I was surprised by the enthusiasm for it. Obviously the situations were the correct form of stimulation.

A week later, more success!

Evaluation

I was very concerned this lesson would not work. However, the pictures offered very good stimulus for conversation. I was amazed at the ideas that came forth about *Werbebild*. *Pirellireifen* certainly caused frustration amongst the girls and prompted them to speak. The boys were lost for words however!

The remaining evaluations come from lessons given to a Year 10 class. It is a class of high ability, but not one entirely without problems, as will become clear.

We find Emma basking in the rewards of teaching. Perhaps it is still the honeymoon period. She is thoughtful about her home-made teaching materials, the quantity of teacher talk compared to pupil talk, and the linguistic progression of the next few lessons.

Evaluation

I enjoyed this class very much. I felt relaxed and confident and able to communicate with ease. The class were attentive and willing to perform the tasks I set. Treatment of the comparative worked well. My flashcards were successful. There was, however, perhaps too much speaking on my part, but the whole lesson was 'presentation' and treatment of new vocabulary/concepts. The production side will have to be in the next three lessons this week.

Here, Emma is thoughtful about her grammar teaching. Old hands might not be surprised at the length of time it takes to grasp the finer points of case morphology. The mood of the class has changed in a very short time; she wonders about this. Add to these worries about the balance of linguistic skills, and pupils' powers of concentration and retention, and one has plenty to think about.

Evaluation

Lesson worked quite well. '*Meiner*' and '*Meine*' concept, however, has not been fully grasped. Needs more practice. Pupils worked well for me, but seemed to have a different 'atmosphere/personality' from the morning. Perhaps less presentation work would be better and more writing and reading the order of the day. I worked them hard. Concentration lapsed a little towards the end. How much of the work has stuck remains to be seen. This is my only concern. Text presentation/listening/writing was good. Oral work? - sloppy.

Here is a satisfying lesson, even though the timing was not quite right. Timing, as Emma is to discover, is very hard. How many of us misjudge it? However, the beginner is more likely to run out of material, and the experienced language teacher, who knows how to squeeze every last drop of benefit from a text or an exercise, is more likely to have something not yet used, when the bell goes.

Evaluation

I only completed Stage 1 and used my back-up, because JA decided to use Stage 2 as part of another lesson. The grammar exercise was quite successful. Students have more of a grasp now of the genitive. It is now only with repeated practice and further examples that it will naturally fall into place and be fully understood. The description exercise came as light relief to the class and incorporated revision of the comparative from Monday's lessons. Thank goodness I had that exercise tucked up my sleeve. The timing just worked out to complete the 35-minute session.

Timing again! Also, we find Emma reflecting about use of the target language. Some lapses into English are hardly surprising.

Emma shows that her language learning objectives are beginning to be realised, but it remains very difficult to motivate her pupils and get them to speak.

Evaluation

Due to lack of time this morning, I completed oral task during this lesson. I recapped on questions and vocab. from this morning and set pupils on task. It worked relatively well. All was in TL, so there was slight confusion at off-set. Some lapses into English, but I think that vocab. for *Selbstbeschreibung* has finally sunk in. Treatment of the results in the grid showed pupils had understood and were able to deal with language needed. Stage 1 - quite successful, but students were reluctant to speak. Stage 2 worked but I only did this exercise orally in class. Pupils seem to be very 'dead' during the afternoons. It's difficult to motivate them. For the last 15 mins, we did *'ich lese gern'* - a good change. An oasis of silence (nearly!) ensued.

Communicating with colleagues is itself a skill. Here, also, we find Emma with a discipline problem. This is what trainees worry about more than anything else. Very understandable, too! However, she is remarkably buoyant about it, even if her self-confidence was slightly dented.

Timing again!

Evaluation

Due to a slight misunderstanding as to whether I should be in the class or not, due to JA being away, I got off to a late start on my lesson. I got the pupils to finish off the written exercises that were set for period 1 and then started on my lesson. Today the class was fine except for Robert A and Iain F. I had to send Robert out in period 1 and in 5 & 6, I sent IF to cool off: too much chattering - that's all. Nothing confrontational. Presentation worked well, but there was no time for a follow up. Oral work will have to be next lesson.

Who would be surprised that Emma was nervous about being observed? (She was probably paralysed with fear when her tutor came to visit.) How reassuring it is to have a colleague who understands the importance of being constructive and giving recognition! Perhaps JA remembers when the roles were reversed.

Evaluation

I was very nervous for this one. Today was the first day I was observed by JA. All went reasonably well. It certainly wasn't my best lesson but J found it acceptable and praised my efforts. She was positive and gave me constructive criticism. Points to note:

- write down resumé on board
- when asking '*was heißt?*' use English, so pupils have to say German back
- write down homework

Timing again! These evaluations which Emma has written show better than any mentor-training where the difficulties of teaching practice lie. In this lesson, additionally, she is coping with pupils' immaturity, the challenge of teaching grammar, and the language teacher's perennial problem, scarcely researched, of how to treat mistakes.

Evaluation

Only got through Stages 1-3. Time did not permit. Method of bringing a pupil out and discussing what he was wearing worked well. *Unterhose* and *Bett* creates great hilarity even though students are 14-15 years old! Genders of clothes is going to prove very difficult. There were lots of mistakes with genders and accusatives. Needs further practice.

All of us feel for Emma when she complains of pupils chattering and giggling. This is a problem for many teachers, but especially corrosive for language teachers, for whom both the content of communications and the means of expressing them must be equally controlled. It makes the task of the trainee very difficult if it is hard to establish good order and enough quiet for the language to be heard. Nevertheless, there are signs of success among the references to difficulties.

Evaluation

Fairly OK. Lesson would have run smoother, had there not been so much fussing in the class - chatter, giggles, etc. JA suggested - instead of *Falsch/richtig* questions (which become monotonous) to try a memory game. *Was trug der Mann* etc. Pupils must try and remember clothes/colours etc. Should work quite well. My attempt lacked pzazz however. The idea was good, but I did not motivate pupils enough by putting whole thing in context, i.e. imagine that you are a witness - the people are criminals, etc. Listening comprehension worked well. Tried elimination game at end - not good. Year 10 obviously didn't catch on. Stage 4 of previous lesson went into this lesson at beginning.

These few laconic statements reveal quite a lot. When a lesson is well timed and pitched at the correct level of difficulty for a class, there is cause for celebration. It seems to have been achieved against the odds, however.

Evaluation

Timing - precise.
Pitch - spot on.
Class management - had to goad and coax students.
Identity parade - worked well. I was very impressed with response.
Mistakes? - didn't speak to Robert at the end of the lesson to tell him off for throwing things.

In the final lesson evaluation of this series, we find Emma still beset with problems of motivation and timing. Judging from my own experiences with a Year 10, it could be a problem for some time to come.

However, the clarity of her reflection and the developing feel for assessing the complexity of language teaching indicate that Emma will be her own very efficient guide and mentor in the future.

Evaluation

Worked quite well. The listening comprehension was a little stilted and pupils were slow to get 'on task' to start the written exercise but it worked however. The adjective exercise was not completed and will have to be done on Wednesday (as a class). I have set the report for local radio as homework.

Emma Taylor is both exceptional and typical of many post-graduate trainees. She is exceptional in the focus and frankness of her self-evaluation. We see not only a fully-justified development of a young teacher's sense of self-worth in the evaluations, but also emerging criteria for that series of professional judgements, which, with isolated exceptions, will have to help her steer her own course throughout a career.

She is typical in encountering the concerns which exercise virtually every trainee for the profession of foreign language teacher: planning, especially timing of lessons, and class management, motivation, and the establishment and maintenance of good behaviour. Through these worries, however, shines the feeling of success at a lesson well-judged and well-delivered. Significantly, these crop up with greater frequency as her teaching practice proceeds. Everyone will hope, with me, that they keep her going.

We are all concerned to find ways of getting pupils to speak fluently and accurately with the widest possible command of the language. In this article, Jacky Ramage takes as a starting point the very intensive reflection on her way of teaching that she did some years ago together with some colleagues in Cleveland. She reviews the effect of that period of reflection five years on, sharing her insights with the reader.

Her principal concern in this article is fluency. She sees pupils' readiness to talk as the key to language proficiency. Accuracy is important, but is something to be developed out of pupils' readiness to speak. A wide-ranging use of the language is also important, but needs the firm base of just a modest amount of language.

Jacky Ramage shares with us her techniques of teaching and her hopes and aspirations for the future.

WORKING TOWARDS FLUENCY
by Jacky Ramage

The experiment

During 1987-88, I was involved in a project co-ordinated by Antony Peck from York's Language Teaching Centre. The aim of the project was to increase the amount of pupil talk in a chosen class - in my case a top set of Year 9. I made careful recordings of my oral practice methods and the amount of time devoted to oral work. After a few weeks of this I made a conscious effort to increase the amount of oral work, to reduce the number of structures introduced or used by the pupils and to aim for greater fluency.

The techniques I used were as follows:

- Teacher-pupil questions and answers
- Pupil-pupil questions and answers
- 'Cued' responses with visual/tactile stimuli
- 'Closed' pair work
- 'Open' pair work
- Pupil-teacher questions
- Pupils taking on the role of teacher
- 'Chains' - where pupils pass questions and answers round the class
- Group work - always with a more able pupil as 'linguistic leader'
- 'On the spot' - where a pupil is asked questions by an audience

These techniques are probably going on in your classroom - and more! What made the difference was the constant and underlying aim to increase pupil talk, reduce the number of structures, increase oral fluency - even to the slight detriment of accuracy, and to remain in the background towards the end of the lesson. Thus support would be gradually withdrawn until pupils were interacting with each other - and I was on 'standby'. The majority of written work was relegated to homework. I thus tried very hard to use as many practice techniques as often as possible.

What happened in the short term?

Exhaustion at first! The amount of time and effort required to plan these lessons took me back to my teaching practice days. However, the effect on my class was amazing. Motivation gradually increased - especially amongst the boys. Accents improved all round. 80-90% of my lessons were oral work and nearly all of the class opted for French in Year 10 - slightly more boys than girls! Traditionally we had always lost the boys to IT and CDT. Two years later, exactly the same number of boys as girls attained A-C grades at GCSE, six went on to study 'A' level French and one pupil is now studying it at university - quite a rarity in rural East Cleveland! This set quite a precedent for male appreciation of languages which continues today.

Five years on

The experiment made a deep impression on me and my pupils. It made me consider certain aspects of my teaching in a radically different way. Those parts of my language teaching which were highlighted by the experiment are ones which I reflect on deeply from year to year and month to month. I am much more aware of everything I am doing in class than I used to be, but certain things I am conscious of all the time. For instance:

- At least 70% of my lessons are oral work and I still ensure that the pupils talk more than I do. I am constantly on the look-out for new and interesting ways to make pupils talk. Greater fluency is a continuous aim. Structures are kept down in number so that the pupils can recall a few with confidence rather than be confused by many.

I reflect also on how to make my teaching as effective with boys as with girls. For instance:

- The motivation of the 'lads' remains a conscious effort. By increasing and practising oral fluency I can capture more male hearts than by being insistent on underlining the date and title. Many boys will be put off by a page of red corrections. The time for insisting on greater accuracy is when they are eating out of your hand.

While some aspects of my teaching have been emphasised, I find that constant review of my practice has led to other changes too. I find I use some techniques less and less. Teacher-pupil questions and choral repetitions can waste time as class sizes increase. Closed pairs are still the most effective way to ensure that everyone 'has a go'.

Further to the demands of the National Curriculum Document and the Higher GCSE role-plays, pupils have to initiate transactions as well as respond to them - make suggestions, open conversations, find out information. New oral materials such as '*Wir Beide*'[1], are reflecting this trend.

---

1   *Wir Beide* Language cards, ISBN 1 897609 00 0, published by Revilo, PO Box 71, Winchester, SO23 8VL.

New strategies

My permanent reflection and review of my oral techniques has resulted in my adopting some new strategies. I have invented/acquired/stolen some more along the way and am pleased to share them with you.

- *Ja/Nein - Oui/Non* Game - pupils must extract pre-determined information from myself or a peer, yet can only receive a yes/no answer. Helps formulation of questions and is good fun.

- Two (newish) routines with flashcards - (a) instead of holding it up for a boring 30 seconds, literally 'flash' it for a second. The pupils may only be able to say *rouge* but, after a few flashes, will be able to describe what they see. (b) Cover up a flashcard and reveal it only gradually. Hands will shoot up to be first! Good for revision.

- Use easily available videos to stimulate oral work - may I recommend Mr Bean and the Chuckle brothers, the latter with the sound turned down. Cheaper than published courses, e.g. *Was hat Herr Bohne gemacht?*

- The concept keyboard can be fun for lower school and special needs. If the monitor is turned away from the keyboard operator then it can become a listening and speaking exercise, and the 'success' noise will tell the pupil he or she is correct. Some published packages such as *Appui*[2] are good - they save time - always important!

- *Gespräche am Flughafen/Conversations à l'Aéroport* - pupils adopt a 'fantasy' identity and destination (the sky's the limit!) and have to move around the classroom chatting each other up and finding out as much as possible.

- *Kategorien/Categories* - fun/oral revision - even for jaded Year 11 GCSE groups. Make a quick list of 40-50 words which fall into categories, e.g. *animal, numéro, meuble, passetemps, autres*, etc. When the word is called out, pupils give the category.

- Team role-plays - good for small groups. E.g. half are the doctor, and half the patient, and they conduct an open role-play. Introduce competition by awarding points for good phrases and ideas and deducting for hesitation.

---

2 *Appui* concept keyboard pack, written by J McElwee and published by Cleveland Educational Computing Centre, Prissick Base, Marton Road, Middlesborough.

Looking to the future

With spoken fluency and confidence a major aim, it is important that oral techniques are revised and refreshed. I find myself thinking critically all the time about how to improve fluency and confidence. This is part of my reflective outlook. It is too easy to 'do' *Tricolore* year after year and become stale. You can become isolated in your classroom, especially in a small school. There should be a Tip Sharing Scheme where local language teachers can get together - perhaps on a commonly arranged PD day. There could be a simple questionnaire beforehand to help identify favourite ideas. The emphasis would be practical.

However, once you have motivated and fluent pupils, the fleeting nature of the six-minute GCSE Speaking Test seems a contradiction. I mark the NEA Speaking Tests and am painfully aware that some candidates have not shown what they are capable of. The Art exams last for two days. Why not languages? The pupils could be recorded towards the end of the session - at their most fluent.

The stage comic asks his partner whether he wants the good news first, or the bad news. The assumption is that both are to come. This chapter has two such messages.

Emma Taylor gives us a vivid picture of how much there is to cope with in language teaching; she reminds us of the many strands of activity and concern that face the beginner. She sees them as individual threads in a Scottish tartan, while the experienced campaigner is more aware of the overall pattern. The 'bad news' is that language teaching, whenever and however we encounter it, is enormously complicated, hard to understand, and difficult to get under control.

Fortunately, there is good news also. Each of the teachers who have written for this chapter shows that intelligence and determination, allied to a sensitive and reflective approach to their work, can lead to improvement and progress. Emma Taylor allows us to see the emergence of professional expertise in its early stages. Jacky Ramage shows that reflection on a specific aspect of teaching can lead to changes in one's method which have permanent, long-term benefits, i.e. her 'reflective teaching'.

Chapter 3

How to reflect?

Confronting the taken-for-granted can often be a source of surprise and a valuable starting point for development. Hearing one's own voice recorded for the first time is a very ordinary case in point. Such familiar features of our lives, looked at from a new angle, can even seem disconcerting at first. So, too, can the photo, letter or diary re-discovered after a passage of time. The surprise, however, can also prompt re-assessment. Are we or were we really like that? Then, if so, what does such insight mean for the directions we now wish to take?

Similarly, there is a whole range of tried and tested procedures which can help to make our taken-for-granted professional activities visible to us in new ways. It is the purpose of this chapter to present examples of that range and of their possible applications; also, to offer some guidance in the matter of choosing what can be of most help to the reflective languages teacher, given his or her particular concerns. Further guidance is provided later, too, in our suggested readings (p88). The books by Allwright (1988), Allwright and Bailey (1991), Brumfit and Mitchell (1990) or Johnstone (1989) may be especially helpful.

Here we need to recognise once more that talk of 'reflective practice' does not imply an assumption that teachers are strangers to thinking about what they do. On the contrary, contemporary teachers have become increasingly self-aware, partly because of the high public profile with which schools now operate, partly and especially because of the planning and co-ordination required of teachers at departmental and school levels, as well as for the classroom. In any case, as previous chapters have emphasised, the taken-for-granted routines of individual lesson planning, discussions with colleagues, etc have always provided opportunities for using experience productively. What is new is the understanding that such reflection can actually provide a refreshing sense of re-gaining control, so long as the procedures themselves are both user-friendly and clearly appropriate.

Procedures for reflection

It may be reassuring to note that the range of possible procedures is not only wide but also includes many which are technically simple. **Diary keeping** is a good example, as Chris and Gill Palmer argue below. So is **mutual observation** by pairs of teachers. That may need nothing more complex than the sharing of each other's observation notes and honest **discussion**; it may on the other hand benefit from use of a well-tried **observation schedule**. Not only is there no single right answer to the question posed in the title of this chapter, but there is no virtue either in a high level of technical sophistication for its own sake. The procedure which is right for a given line of enquiry is simply the most appropriate one for that task; and many procedures of great potential value require little more than trial and error to become fruitful.

Reassurance can also be taken from the fact that a lot of valuable classroom studies have begun without any very precise 'research' agenda. Indeed, if teachers' reflection is to contain maximum potential for innovation and not simply be tied to the agenda of others, the open-ended start must remain a valid option. Where reflection is not clearly focused at the outset, there are various ways into open-ended inquiry which can be tried out.

*Re-scanning a run of diary entries covering a previous period, for instance, can provide a fresh perspective on other entries of which one has more recent memory and can thus open up new lines of thought. **Audio** or **video** recording can be another useful starting point, as suggested by John Batey and David Westgate in this chapter. Making a brief **descriptive log** of what has been recorded may bring ideas and questions to the surface. The process of choosing a passage to transcribe, and then of deciding what ought to be included in the transcript, is even more likely to do so. Similarly, the practice of reciprocal (or peer) observation, as described by Eryl Griffiths later in this chapter, can also reveal aspects of teachers' or pupils' behaviour which are new to those involved, though she does go on to suggest that this technique may be best suited to providing data on already defined questions.*

The point is that useful reflection may start in open-ended ways, gaining precision as the work proceeds. On the other hand, each of the techniques mentioned here may be just the one to serve purposes clearly in focus from the start. Christine Korczak, for instance, our final contributor to this chapter, approached her reflective inquiry with an issue of great current interest already very clearly in view. She wanted to investigate the extent to which the target language was being used in lessons and found an observation schedule approach most appropriate. She describes the design and use of observation schedules (for so-called 'systematic observation') and the kinds of practical decisions which are involved in making the chosen instrument most revealing.

We begin, however, with the 'low-tech' diary: its potential and procedures for its use. In the following contribution, Chris and Gill Palmer begin by describing the rationale and origins of diary keeping as a form of reflective data. They go on to distinguish various possible uses for such data and some issues to which these can give rise. They draw on personal experience and share some general conclusions.

Diary keeping and reflecting on practice
by Chris and Gill Palmer

The diary or journal has become a basic tool in enabling the learner or teacher to reflect on classroom experience. Just as one might keep a diary to record the events of one's everyday life, so a learner or teacher keeps a diary to record classroom events, in order to understand better the processes involved. Bailey (1990) describes the diary as:

> *A first-person account of a language learning or teaching experience, documented through regular, candid entries in a personal journal and then analysed for recurring patterns of salient events* (p215).

The diary is usually kept on a daily or weekly basis and records the events of a lesson and individual reactions to and perceptions of those events. The act of documenting what takes place in the classroom allows the author to reflect back on learning and teaching behaviour and in so doing to clarify thoughts, or to analyse and evaluate progress; the diary thus provides a personalised sounding board. Taking a step back from the immediate event often allows one greater awareness and insights, especially if the diary is kept over a period of time. The process of recording, reviewing and reflecting may enable one to perceive what may otherwise be hidden from view. A teacher taking part in a study reported in Lowe (1987) remarked that:

> *I have been teaching for ten years, making assumptions about how my students felt, which ones were nervous and which ones weren't, and it's really rather frightening for me to realise how much was going on, important things that were happening to people in the class, that I really didn't know about.*

Diaries in educational research

Diaries have had their place in educational research since the early 1970s. In particular, they have been used in classroom-centred research to get inside what Long (1980) calls 'the black box', namely, to find out what really takes place in the classroom, or:

> to document what actually was involved in our attempts to learn... second languages... Daily events and thoughts and feelings related to them were recorded in a log-like fashion. We each then went through our own data and tried to identify the important variables affecting our language learning.
>
> (Schumann, 1980, p51)

These pioneering diaries afforded insights into **learner** variables such as eavesdropping (versus speaking) as a language learning strategy; also into **teacher** variables such as preference for a teacher-dominated classroom.

More recently, diaries have been adopted by teachers as a means of carrying out action research into what works and what does not work in their classrooms and why (see Lowe, 1987; Palmer G, 1992). Sometimes this device may be incorporated into pre-service (Thornbury, 1991) or in-service training (Palmer C, 1992) and may thus be formalised as a means of consciousness raising and self-evaluation. However, the diary is also becoming increasingly widespread as a simple means of self-monitoring for the classroom practitioner. The resulting insights are more likely to be reported in a staff meeting or teachers' newsletter or kept for personal reflection than reported to the world at large. The diary has also been used increasingly since the early 80s in conjunction with other means of observation and monitoring, such as self-reporting, interviews, questionnaires and audio and video recordings (see Nunan, 1989; Allwright and Bailey, 1991).

Diaries and effective teaching

Diaries can thus be used in a variety of ways to help learners and teachers reflect on the language teaching process.

- HOW LEARNERS LEARN
  Firstly, they can help us to understand how learners learn. It is possible through the diary technique for learners to reflect on how they learn and thus to uncover those factors which influence learning. These may include expectations, goals, styles, strategies and motivation, for example. Keeping a daily or weekly diary can also enable students to monitor their learning progress and, in raising their awareness of how they learn, help them to become more efficient learners.

- Effects of teaching on learning
Secondly, diaries may be used to investigate the effect teaching has on learning. Through student and teacher diaries, factors influencing teaching and classroom behaviour which may not readily be perceived on the surface may be uncovered. The diary may thus be used as a tool to help the teacher investigate such variables as teacher talk, classroom management, lesson planning and structuring, materials, tasks and activities used, etc. Diaries may also be used to understand the classroom crucible of group dynamics and the factors which influence the way the class operates as a unit. Influential factors might include the timetable, the range of backgrounds and interests of the learner group, teacher-student and student-student relationships, or varying preferences for teaching style and classroom organisation.[1]

- Record of classroom practice
Thirdly, diaries can help teachers and trainee teachers to develop their ability to observe, review and assess their classroom practice, whether they rely on their own diary keeping or include that of learners and/or outside observers. Student teachers may use the diary to help guide them through the ups and downs of teaching practice, where learning through reflection is an essential component. Teachers on in-service courses may use diaries to reflect on specific aspects of their teaching in relation to the course content, or simply to capitalise on the opportunity which the course should provide to reflect on issues of teaching and learning away from immediate teaching pressures. Diaries can provide a means of monitoring and evaluation for all teachers when a problem arises in a class, when they are introducing new techniques and materials, when a classroom event strikes them as interesting or unusual. Teachers can use log-keeping either on an informal, personal basis or as part of more extended, advanced forms of action research.

Diaries: organisation and implementation

So far we have considered the use of diaries for reflection; we go on to look at some of the issues of their organisation and implementation. The first question to be addressed by the author/researcher is who exactly the participants in the diary project will be. To a certain extent this will depend on the circumstances. If a diarist wishes to investigate his or her own language learning in a particular environment, this may well necessitate a solitary journal. However, diarists may find other learners in the same circumstances, and will have to decide whether to keep their diary independently or in conjunction with the other students. Where the student is learning in a formal classroom situation, all the learners may be asked to keep diaries.

---

1   These are areas in which diaries can reveal deep and important feelings (Eds).

The main advantage of writing alongside others is that a second stage of corroboration of data is added to the diary writing project. Learners compare their experiences and gain further perspectives on the learning process and classroom behaviours and events in so doing. This process is known as **triangulation**, a concept with its roots in ethnography. Its advantages are not only gaining further insights from others and thus forming a more complete picture of the teaching and learning taking place, but through comparison, clarifying insights and thinking processes. The disadvantages hinge on whether a diarist wishes to show or discuss what may be an intimate medium with fellow students or the teacher. The process of triangulation may also be a time-consuming process; the scope and purpose of the project may determine whether this aspect is included.[2]

Teachers on an in-service course where a diary project was run by Palmer G (1992) elected to write a joint diary; other innovations have included alternating diary writing with discussion groups and using them in conjunction with methodology notebooks (Hundleby and Breet, 1988). The issue of time may again influence teachers in deciding whether to keep a solitary journal when reflecting on their classroom teaching, or whether also to invite students simultaneously to write diaries which are then monitored by the teacher for corroborative purposes. Other outside observers may also be involved in diary projects, whether they are peer teachers, tutors or teaching advisers. Certainly, a triangulation approach requiring both teacher and pupils to keep diaries will ensure a more balanced and reliable set of data to work from, but this may also raise other issues, such as confidentiality (see below), which the teacher may wish to avoid.

Figure 1

Triangulation and differences of perspective

These diary entries were all written by participants in the same event!

First, comments from four of the students:

> I did not understand all of the text because it is a topic I know little about. I would certainly have had difficulties in understanding it in Norwegian too. We discussed it and talked it over in our group. That made it clearer and easier to remember the main points.

---

2 It can also provide some thought-provoking differences of view. See, for instance, figure 1, based upon data provided by Chris and Gill Palmer (Eds).

I got nervous when speaking in the bigger group - difficult to express yourself when you don't understand what the opinion of the party was.

Because of my short time studying English, I felt quite uncertain and uncomfortable and didn't participate in the discussion very much. But I feel I learned.

Everybody had to talk. We enjoyed it. There was a lot of 'organised noise'. We learnt new words and we learnt about British politics.

An observer's view:

They spent quite a long time reading and had some difficulty explaining it to the other people when we exchanged information.

...the text was very difficult, maybe too difficult. The teacher could have been more active.

And finally the teacher wrote:

Both groups found the reading difficult. Although they said this, they seemed to have drawn out the main points... The exercise created a lot of discussion... very positive in feedback at the end, saying they like the way of working and found it interesting.

A significant variety for the teacher to reflect on - and perhaps to take further in discussion - for instance, with the students.

Naturalistic and interventionist approaches

A second question concerns ways in which the approach adopted by a diarist will influence the quantity and quality of the data and its potential benefit for self-reflection. There are two main approaches - naturalistic and interventionist. When a **naturalistic** approach is used, the diarist writes on anything which appears to be significant when reflecting on a classroom event and its outcomes. With an **interventionist** approach, more control is exerted over the content of the diaries. The diarist selects an area for investigation which may be more or less precise, such as group dynamics, using listening tasks in the classroom, giving instructions or questioning techniques. While an interventionist approach will focus the mind on a particular area or areas of interest, and thus produce more material of direct relevance, it is argued that this may result in apparently peripheral yet ultimately significant reflections being dismissed as irrelevant. Conversely, particularly with an untrained learner or diarist, the naturalistic approach can produce a preponderance of trivia or confused comment. The issue then arises of the extent to which a teacher/tutor should give guidance and direction to learners and trainees undertaking a diary project. Again, it is the purpose of the diary project and the needs of the learners or teachers in question which will decide what approach is adopted.

Ownership of findings

The third main issue is ownership of the findings. Diaries are normally very personal vehicles of introspection and self-reflection. The findings may arouse strong feelings and be very revealing, yet at the same time very damaging to the individual teacher or student unless handled appropriately. This raises the question of anonymity and confidentiality. If a diary is to be read by one or more people besides the author, then the diarist may wish to remain anonymous or may ask for a guarantee of confidentiality. A diarist may also wish to edit a diary before it is read by others, perhaps keeping the original, personal version but allowing highlights for more public consumption, or rewriting or summarising before release. If a diary is written in the knowledge that others will read it, it is likely that a degree of self-censorship and even self-flattery may enter into the writing, particularly if the reader is perceived as being in a position of authority. A fear of exposure or risk of humiliation may, in fact, deter the diarist from candid introspection and undermine the purpose of log-keeping. It is clear that permission should always be sought from a diarist before their journal is given to other readers, and that great care should be taken in collection, analysis and possible publication of the findings.

The journal is proving to be a highly flexible and adaptable tool. The purpose, format and organisation may vary from a solitary journal which is naturalistic and introspective to a joint or group diary focusing on specific issues of learning or teaching. The impetus for writing a diary may be private, instigated by an individual for others, a group enterprise or a means of public appraisal. It may be written on a daily, weekly or occasional basis and range from a stream of consciousness to highly edited telegrammatic notes. First and foremost, its relevance lies in the insights it can offer through observation and reflection, allowing learners greater confidence to develop their learning potential, or teachers further room for professional growth. The opportunity to take a second look, stand back and review the learning and teaching process, is engendering a wealth of new information about what really goes on in the classroom.

Diaries indisputably provide data on the perceptions of those participating in the teaching or learning process, data which are especially revealing when those of different participants in the same event are compared, or 'triangulated'. Video data, on the other hand, might be thought much more objective; surely, as the cliché has it, the camera cannot lie. Perhaps not. It cannot capture everything, however, nor see behind its subject. Microphones also have their limitations; they cannot capture group-sound, but only one speaker at a time. Otherwise, they simply produce an incomprehensible blur. Teacher or pupil subjects have to some extent to be targeted separately or grouped in some way. Both video and audio recordings are for such reasons inevitably selective. They also work with observable behaviour and do not (indeed, cannot) seek to explain what they do capture. There ought, therefore, to be no great surprise in finding users of video recordings also emphasising the importance of the insider's view in making sense of their data. These self-same reasons, however, underline the suitability of audio or video recording as the starting point for open-ended enquiry as well as for defined studies.

It is with attempts to create the circumstances for detached analysis and open-mindedness that John Batey and David Westgate begin their account which follows next. A main theme concerns procedures which brought to the discussion of transcribed lesson extracts the views of a group of three or four practitioners whose insider knowledge varied in extent or quality simply by virtue of their role in relation to the events transcribed: i.e. in turn as teacher, co-teacher, observer, sound-recordist or just departmental colleague.

VIDEO ACTION REPLAY
by John Batey and David Westgate

Picture the scene: a sunny garden one afternoon in early summer; 9C have just dispersed to their individual identities; chilled white wine, congenial company, time to reflect. Strange but true, we were working! Admittedly, only an escape from the physical confines of school had enabled us to establish some needed objective distance. (It was not, as sceptics might have suggested, a flight from an alcohol-free zone! Well, not entirely.) Modern schools are, alas, often frantic places and the decision to reflect on practice must be firm, definite and determined. Our 'escape' on this occasion, sweet in the memory, was a physical reflection of that fact. We were in our second round of gathering and analysing video data (1988) and we were getting wise. We had already spent (twilight) time in school viewing and discussing the videos, so we could now lay the technology to one side and deal more closely with the transcripts (videos? transcripts? flashback mode!).

Making transcripts

All transcripts are potentially very rich in matters for comment and deserve some time and care. Even the simplest take time to prepare after all. They can contain lots of additional detail, from marks showing how speakers pause or how loudly they speak, through to elaborate symbols for coding each utterance, e.g. showing a speaker initiating an exchange, evaluating a previous utterance and so on. (For technical guidance readers would need to consult, for instance, Allwright and Bailey, 1991; Brumfit and Mitchell, 1990; Nunan, 1989; or Edwards and Westgate, 1987.) However, at the simpler end of the spectrum, transcripts may be little different from a play-script, just showing who speaks and what is said.

For most purposes, the reflective languages teacher needs nothing very complicated: just the speakers, the 'text' and a few contextual notes (e.g. for the wink or smile which suggests that the speaker should not be taken literally just then). Teachers and pupils, like anyone else, do not always mean what they appear to say. For instance, a teacher may on some occasion use quite strong words, appearing to call a pupil foolish, but speak in a certain tone, with a certain facial expression and invoking previously stated high expectations, which together actually imply a general judgement which is the exact opposite of what was said. Teachers reading a transcript extract together draw on what they know their classrooms are often like, a 'shared professional culture' to put it grandly. They usually identify likely meanings and read easily between the lines, though we certainly changed our initial interpretation once or twice in the process of discussion. One such case involved a pupil-provoked series of teasing exchanges between teacher and class in English, amid teacher-led oral French. First tempted to think the pupils were not following the teacher's agenda, we came subsequently to see these pupils' activity at this point as no more than 'having a bit of fun' and gaining some breathing space in their own terms. (An extract of this transcript is given as Figure 2, below.) Collective attempts to make sense of transcripts are rarely boring and can often be challenging or disturbing. At least, that has been our experience.

Discussing transcripts

Our transcripts began simple, though we tended to scribble in plenty of notes on our xeroxed copies as discussions developed. We needed to collect ideas about what we thought was going on at a level of detail impossible to catch except by this kind of retrospection; also about the possible significance of what the teacher or pupils said or did. For us, these discussions of the transcripts were a natural step from seeing each other's lessons and from shared viewing of the videos; of course they also drew heavily on our trusting relationship which had grown out of all that. We needed the trust in order to begin to evaluate each other's performance: a lack of pace for one of us, rather heavy feedback in oral work (always repeating the pupil's response) for another, and so on. We had also by this time shown some of the videos (not all twelve or so hours!) to classes concerned. Their responses, as well as their informed memories (e.g. about who had been speaking off-camera, or about a joke not shared with the teacher at the time) helped greatly in widening our understanding of particular sections of lessons and of processes involved.

Useful, too, were the sound-only interviews with the teachers, made immediately after the lessons. These were especially useful in capturing impressions as to the typicality of events just recorded. (The possible distortion of 'normality' due simply to the fact of being recorded has to be faced.) The interviews focused helpfully, too, on aspects of the lesson which had been adapted from the intended plan. Such statements could be drawn on as some kind of objective data at the discussion stage.

Figure 2

(NB: Italicised phrases within square brackets are translations and not part of the dialogue)

Line	Speaker	Text	Pragmatics
1	T	Après cela... après cela... after	Writes après cela
2		that... après cela... after that	on board; addresses
3	Ps	(chatter)	all Ps, inc. some by
4	T	So we've got d'abord... [*first*]	board. Points to P1

Line	Speaker	Text	Pragmatics
5	P1	Je prends un... une doche.	(In group at front).
6	T	Une dou...	Grins.
7	Ps	Douche. (some comment) [shower]	
8	T	Douche... Puis...? Je... [Then...? I...]	Points to P2 (also at
9	P2	Je me lave les cheveux. [Wash my hair]	front).
10	T	Puis...?	Points to P3 (also at
11	P3	Je fouais ma toilette. [Have a wash]	front). (Error 2nd word)
12	T	Je fais ma toilette... et après cela...	To class.
13		... Now what do you do after that?	
14	P4	Brush your teeth.	At front.
15	Ps	(Various comments, inc.: Have your	Class as a whole.
16		breakfast first)	
17	T	Don't you have your breakfast before	
18		you brush your teeth?	
19	Ps	No! (etc)	
20	T	Eugh!	Grimaces.
21	Ps	(Various comments)	
22	T	Do you come to school with bits of	Appearing horrified.
23		cornflakes and bacon in your teeth?	
24	Ps	Yeah! (etc)	
25	T	Oh you horrible lot!	Grimaces.
26	Ps	(Various, inc.: I have my breakfast	Some laughter.
27		first; I don't brush my teeth at all)	
28	T	You don't brush your teeth at all?	To individual boy.
29		Ah, well, if he doesn't brush his teeth	To class, over various
30		at all, right, I mean, that's completely	chatter.
31		different... Come on then,	Grins.
32		what are we going to have after this?	
33	P5	Brush your hair.	Offering.
34	Ps	Brush your hair. Yeah.	Agreeing.
35	T	Brush your hair, OK... So what's	
36		that then?	
37	P6	Je me brosse... [I brush my...]	
38	T	Je me brosse...	
39	Ps	Le... (etc)	
40	P	Les cheveux. [hair]	
41	T	Les cheveux... OK.	Accepts offer.
42	P6	Je me brosse les cheveux.	
43	T	Right.	

There are many questions raised by such a transcript. Few are better placed to answer them than colleagues who know the teacher and the class.

Insights gained from transcripts

First time round (back in 1983) we had been struck by how teacher-prescribed so much of the classroom activity had been. The videos had revealed emotional responses of the children to the lessons and to each other; also their lack of physical freedom (which the MFL department subsequently tried to address). The transcripts fixed not so much the linguistic details and structure as transactional data and language. We recognised how central the teacher had to be as a language model, but had not realised the degree to which the teachers dominated organisational and teaching transactions as well as classroom space. Without the overlay of transcript on video, we doubt whether this possibly stultifying aspect of social interaction in foreign language classrooms would have leapt out so starkly at us. Anyway, by the time we came to make our second set of recordings it was what the pupils themselves were making of all our efforts which emerged as the central line to pursue, and we needed to look closely at what their contributions might really mean. As described above and elsewhere (Westgate et al, 1990), our preliminary individual attempts to interpret transcripts were sometimes severely revised, and quite fresh insights were arrived at, through the process of discussing them.

It is probably clear by this point that the lessons we recorded were never intended to be regarded as models; they were simply part of a cyclical programme of reflection. The recordings themselves were seen as potential sources of evidence which would help us clarify questions which teaching together was already suggesting. Thus they were not the absolute starting point, and it was possible to prepare for them in the sense of getting pupils used to having more than one adult around at a time, used even to the recording equipment via a 'dry run' lesson or two. Recordings have nevertheless been used subsequently for some training purposes, e.g. with PGCE students, as starting points for discussion or as illustrating one of many ways in which teachers can approach aspects of their work. So it is just as well that our 'collaborative action research' - for that, we were to discover, was the name of our game - has always been inherently hostile towards easy answers and fanciful or sweeping generalisations. We would readily admit that considered answers even to such apparently trivial questions as: 'Why did you raise your eyebrow there?' became significant in our discussions about, for example, reward and support for pupils during teacher-pupil exchanges.

Hence the importance to us of our sunny afternoon. Watching oneself and colleagues on video is inevitably a somewhat subjective spectator sport. Often only distance can provide the necessary degree of objectivity. We happened that day to choose distance in the physical and social as well as the more usual temporal and intellectual terms. Our critical faculties seemed to have been sharpened, judging by the amount of traditional red pen on the transcripts by the end. We were no doubt also trying to practise what we preached about use of space and truly interactional exchanges which involve much soul-searching -

enlivened this time, though, by little echoes of those café set lessons we videotaped: *Un petit vin blanc, monsieur?*

In the next contribution, Eryl Griffiths describes long-standing personal experience of EFL teachers observing each other's lessons in various supportive ways. She stresses not only the gains in practical understanding which those taking part often derive from peer observation, but also the potentially strong feelings involved and the sensitivity which these require. Issues of relative status and power can also cause unforeseen difficulties. She concludes with some thoughts on circumstances in which peer observation can have optimum value.

KEEPING AN EYE ON EACH OTHER: PEER OBSERVATION
by Eryl Griffiths

My starting point with peer observation was the production of an article entitled 'Autonomy and teacher learning' in 1988. Katie Shaw, teacher trainer at the Lee Green Eurocentre, Frank Heyworth, Director of Operations at our Head Office in Zürich, and I began from the idea that if 'learner autonomy', 'self-study skills', etc were important concepts in how to help increasingly sophisticated students learn English as a foreign language, then surely they must be important concepts in teacher learning. As old lags at the ELT game we felt needs to:

- update/deepen/polish up our skills and knowledge;
- counter the isolation of the classroom;
- access non-threatening, meaningful, focused feedback;
- get the training we wanted when we wanted it and not be at the mercy of what happened to be on offer from suppliers of one-day/one-week training courses;
- work with our own colleagues in our own schools.

We came up with the idea of a menu of packs, created by and for teachers within our organisation. Each pack would be a resource base for six or more hours of in-service development work to be undertaken by individuals, dyads, or small groups of teachers. The packs would be open-ended; those who worked with them would also add to them. They were meant to support sustained attention to a particular area, in contrast to one-off lectures or workshops which had hitherto characterised our INSET programme.

Peer observation pack

The first pack put together was the peer observation pack. It contained pre-observation paraphernalia: background and theoretical articles (and summaries of these for the short-of-time), discussion documents on how and why peer observation can be useful and invigorating, points to be borne in mind when planning an observation cycle, guidelines for negotiating sensitive areas like the 'contract of confidentiality' between peer observers. It contained post-observation props: debriefing and evaluation questionnaires, invitations to write up reports of the experience and feed them back into the initial reading for the next round of peer observation.

The pack was trialled at the Lee Green Eurocentre. Here are some extracts from the feedback collected there. One teacher said:

> *I felt threatened by the idea of having someone observe me for so many lessons and I thought I'd lose confidence, but in fact the observations had the opposite effect - they gave my confidence a boost and, at the same time, I felt they were helping me to keep on my toes. Instead of feeling threatened, I felt that my partner was giving me a great deal of support.*

Another said:

> *I felt that by watching other teachers teach, I started seeing much more in other people's teaching, and I found that I have become much more receptive to comments about my teaching because I perceive them to be constructive rather than critical.*

One teacher, who had become used to requesting his peer partner to focus and comment on specific aspects of a lesson, went on to make the same kind of request to the principal when the evaluative observation was due. He asked the principal to look particularly at his blackboard work and at lesson phasing. This teacher initiative 're-cast' the usually rather tense evaluative observation with its judgement day atmosphere into something closer to collaboration between two professionals.

The pack has been used as a basis for successive waves of peer observation at the Cambridge Eurocentre. In 1990 we became interested in the notion that we might have been rather glib in our use of the term 'peer'. That is, we had assumed that observations between teachers, as opposed to those involving principal/director of studies/senior teacher, were automatically peer observations. In fact, differences in age, experience, gender, qualifications, personality, special interests and areas of expertise can all be perceived as introducing hierarchical elements into what is supposed to be a self-help procedure between equals. We felt unable to take account of all these elements, but we did take a small step towards greater sensitivity that summer when Tony Robinson, a senior teacher, facilitated peer observations between our temporary summer teachers, a mainly young, relatively inexperienced, enormously enthusiastic bunch of people. They appreciated the sharing with each other and the privacy from the permanent teachers which this approach entailed.

In 1991 we stumbled on another area of strong and peer group support feelings - the external enemy. We decided to organise a wave of four peer observations per teacher (seeing and being seen) prior to our three-yearly inspection by the British Council. The original idea was just to get over the strangeness of having an 'outsider' in one's classroom so that having an inspector there would not feel like such a big deal. We were aiming simply to be over first-night stage fright before the inspectors came, but found that this round of peer observation was particularly rich in exchange of teaching ideas, tips, mutual support and encouragement. Incidentally, the inspection also went off well.

I would not like to give the impression that our peer observation pack has been in constant use over all these years and that every member of staff is fully conversant with all its contents. Nevertheless, some peer observations do take place. By and large, they are found thought-provoking and enjoyable by participants. Months go by; everyone forgets about peer observation and focuses on something else, then it re-emerges as a methodology for a term's INSET.

Some possible problems

This appears to be a widespread pattern. I gave a paper on our peer observation experiences at the British Council Conference in Milan in 1992, and the Italian state school teachers there reported similar cycles. Everyone likes peer observation in theory but, in practice, organisational difficulties (timetabling, cover, etc) and some sort of personal reticence seem to conspire to prevent it taking place very often. These impressions were also confirmed by the small group who met to discuss peer observation at the IATEFL conference in Swansea this year (1993). Peer observation is a good idea, **but**... seems to be the general message. Many have tried it once or twice, but I have not been able to find fully-fledged teachers who have lengthy/in-depth experience of using peer observation as a tool for personal or pedagogical development. I would be extremely interested to hear from anyone who has.

Where it may fit in

My current hypothesis is that, in our attempt to break down teacher isolation, peer observation is not necessarily a good **first** step. Organisationally and personally, team teaching is far easier to get up and running; it is less threatening and more fun. The place for peer observation would seem to be where teachers who are already confident about working together have a 'puzzle' about some aspect of classroom life and a conviction that peer observation would help them solve it, i.e. where the peer observers themselves have both the focus to make it useful and the motivation to make it happen.

Finally, Christine Korczak describes the principles and practice of schedule-based observation of classroom events. She emphasises the adaptability of the approach and provides some guidance concerning the practical decisions affecting its fine-tuning for the purposes it is designed to serve.

USING AN OBSERVATION SCHEDULE
by Christine Korczak

For several years now, I have been fascinated by the challenge of increasing the amount of the target language which I use in my own foreign language teaching. When I had the opportunity to visit other classrooms in my LEA as part of a one-year secondment in 1989-90, I chose the use of the target language as the main focus of my lesson observations.

The benefits of using the target language as 'the principal means of communication', as outlined in the Non-statutory Guidance for Modern Foreign Languages in the National Curriculum (1992), are now widely recognised though, for various reasons, frequently not achieved. I wanted to find out the extent to which the target language was being used, as opposed to English, by teachers and pupils in classes similar to my own, and to see if there were lessons to be learned for my own practice.

Systematic observation

As I was interested in the proportions of target language and English used in other teacher's classrooms, I carried out extensive observations in which I used a 'systematic' rather than random approach. For the sake of convenience, I hoped to be able to use an existing observation schedule which had been specifically designed for observing foreign language classes. The Nearhoof Adaptation observation schedule (1969; cited in Allwright, 1988) seemed at first to be ideal for my purpose as it had categories for both teacher and student talk.

However, as some of the categories of the original schedule were rather ambiguous, I modified them and produced my own Nearhoof Adaptation schedule. My version deliberately contained an equal number of categories for student talk and teacher talk. This was because I was equally interested in the students' and the teacher's use of the foreign language. I also made a clear distinction between the use of the target language for the purpose of 'real communication' (i.e. for the genuine exchange of meaning) and for 'practice' (i.e. any exercises mainly to do with practising details).

Use of first or foreign language

The topic of target language use lends itself very readily to being investigated by techniques of systematic classroom observation. These allow use of either target language or mother tongue to be quantified in terms of the frequency with which each is noted at set intervals of time. I chose the arbitrary time unit of three seconds, which enabled me to get a quite precise picture of the use of the target language and English in the observed lessons. These were all at beginners' level, a phase which interests me because it is one in which attitudes to learning and use are being formed. It is sometimes argued that target language use is easier and more valuable with more advanced students; in my view, it is more significant early on.

Using an observation schedule

I used the following equipment in my lesson observations:

- a copy of the Nearhoof Adaptation schedule;
- a pen and some lined paper on which to write the different categories of the schedule and my field notes;
- a walkman with a C-90 cassette of pre-recorded three-second bleeps.

I usually sat as unobtrusively as I could at the back of the classroom. I had one ear-piece of my walkman in one ear and listened to the bleeps. With my other ear I listened to what was taking place in the lesson. I simply noted down a category from my schedule every time I heard a bleep. During extended periods of the same type of lesson activity, I followed the instructions of the schedule, writing down the category which described the activity and drawing a continuous line underneath it until a change of activity occurred. I was thus free to write field notes about any notable aspects of the lesson. These were to give me important background information about the activities or structure of the lesson.

Additional data

My field notes complemented the quantitative data for each lesson. I also collected material such as worksheets, made a note of any coursebooks which were used, and I administered a questionnaire (structured interview) to find out background information about the teachers. To give what I hoped would be a fair picture, I observed at least four lessons by each teacher.

From the outset, I told the teachers whom I was going to observe that the focus of my observation would be the use which they and their pupils made of the target language. I felt that I had to explain why I would be sitting there with my walkman and with one ear-piece in my ear! I also did not want them to think I was recording their whole lessons. I decided that the teachers' knowledge of my focus would be unlikely to have a significant effect either on the course of the events observed or the data which I would derive from them. I was confident of this because of the nature of the topic I was investigating. Since use of the target language as 'the normal means of communication' has to be built up over a period of time, I felt I could assume that, if a teacher suddenly started using a large amount of target language after previously using mainly English, the students would probably make their surprise or lack of comprehension quite obvious.

At the end of each lesson I had several columns of hand-written letters and figures which represented the sequence of events. As I eventually observed over 110 lessons, it was practical for the data to be typed into a computer. By using a computer program, I could produce a matrix showing the use of target language and English in each lesson. Data from the matrix could then be displayed in the form of bar charts and reveal differences from lesson to lesson. Figures 3 and 4 show the categories of the Nearhoof Adaptation schedule and bar charts for four teachers. Both diagrams are concerned with oral interaction (speaking) and reflect the categories of the matrix. Although the full version of the schedule contains additional categories for 'Type of skill' and 'Type of interaction', I am concentrating here on verbal interaction alone.

What the observation schedule revealed

The observations confirmed that it is possible to use the target language as the 'principal means of communication'. There were some excellent examples amongst the observed teachers and their students, as can be seen in the bar charts (Figure 4). These teachers were not limited to a particular language; between them they taught French, German and Spanish. Similarly, examples of low-level use of target language (by teacher and students) were found in all three languages.

In the lessons I observed, there were frequent examples of teacher-student and student-teacher use of the target language. However, there were few instances of student-student use for 'real communication' - as, for example, one occasion recorded in my field notes when a student did spontaneously ask another for a rubber in French: *Puis-je avoir une gomme?*

The teachers who used the target language most extensively were characterised by their personal commitment to its normal use. There appeared to be no correlation between the teachers' formal qualifications in the foreign language and their use of it for teaching. I observed teachers who had recently attended a

'Spanish from scratch' course as part of an LEA initiative to implement the diversification of language teaching in schools. One of these teachers, who taught Spanish to Year 7 pupils, used the target language almost exclusively. It is interesting that this teacher (Teacher A in Figure 4), who had himself only learned Spanish for less than a year, spoke even more of the target language in his lessons than did a graduate teacher of Spanish (Teacher D). Teacher A was also older than the graduate teacher, which illustrates that target language use is independent of the teacher's age (and youth!) as well.

Figure 3

Nearhoof Adaptation observation schedule (1990)

Type of verbal interaction (Speaking)

1. Teacher use of language for 'real communication'
   - foreign language   1F
   - English   1E

2. Teacher use of language for 'practice'
   - foreign language   2F
   - English   2E

3. Student use of language for 'real communication'
   - foreign language   3F
   - English   3E

4. Student use of language for 'practice'
   - foreign language   4F
   - English   4E

0. Non-interactive activities, e.g. silence, etc.

The use of language for 'real communication' refers to the genuine exchange of meaning. For the teacher, this includes the language which is used for classroom management. For the student(s), this includes any occasion on which language is used spontaneously.

The use of language for 'practice' refers to any type of 'practice' exercise. For the teacher, this includes the occasions on which the language is used to correct student errors. For the student(s), this includes the occasions on which previously introduced structures (oral or written) are recalled and recombined to form acceptable responses.

Figure 4

Bar charts summarising all lessons of four observed teachers

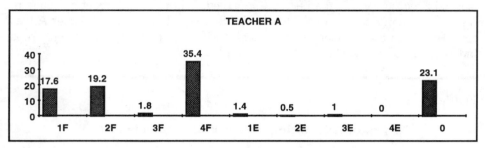

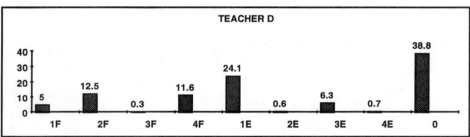

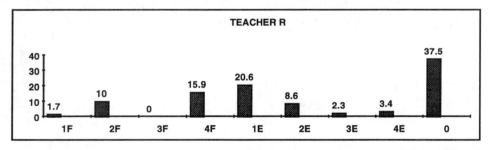

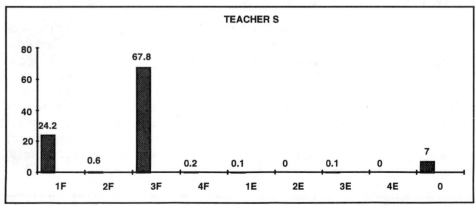

Strengths and limitations

At all stages of my classroom observations, I was aware of the limitations as well as the strengths of observation schedules. Their use has to be combined with other methods (e.g. interviews) if you want to know more about a teacher's reasons for teaching in one way or another. Systematic observation naturally prevents you from observing all aspects of the rich variety of phenomena which are present in language classrooms. My schedule, for instance, takes no account of non-verbal behaviour in the form of mime or gesture; nor does it comment upon turn-taking. Such a device focuses your attention and measures what you have chosen to look at. In my case, the matrices and bar charts gave me simply and exactly the kind of information I needed in order to compare and contrast target language use across a range of lessons.

You may be wondering, however, which (if any) of these bar charts would resemble your own teaching. If you monitored yourself, you would probably be surprised. The results might also give you an incentive to increase your use of the target language. If that were your long-term goal, you could at first adopt bit-by-bit strategies, deciding that you and your pupils were going to make a sustained effort over short stretches of time, for instance. Halliwell and Jones (1991) suggest giving an instruction such as *X Minuten auf Deutsch*, and allowing no English during that time. Your longer-term strategies might involve periodic self-monitoring of the kind I have described, co-opting the help of colleagues or working on recordings of your own lessons. If you and your colleagues were to apply systematic observation techniques to one another's lessons from time to time, you might be able to plot some dramatic changes!

This chapter has included accounts of four quite different ways of reflecting, with advice about the potential value and possible limitations of each. Two related themes have been evident throughout: first, the reassurance for the novice which is to be found in the variety of useful techniques available, most of which are relatively simple to operate; and, second, the emphasis upon appropriateness to circumstance and purpose as the most important guide to choice of procedure. Each approach can claim to bring aspects of teaching and learning into clearer focus. In the chapter which follows, we turn our attention to the outcomes of selected projects through which language teachers have reflected upon aspects of their work.

Chapter 4

What outcomes may we expect?

Attempts made during the 1960s and 1970s to make global comparisons of language teaching methodology in order to discover the most effective were almost all inconclusive. This applied to the famous comparison of the audio-lingual method with the traditional method (Scherer and Wertheimer, 1964), and to the GUME experiment (Gothenberg-Teaching-Methods-English) of 1968, described by Levin (1972) and to a number of other projects and experiments. This general failure led Allwright to say (Allwright, 1972): 'I would like to claim therefore, that the problem of description is a fundamental problem in research on language teaching'. This point of view was echoed by David Stern ten years later (Stern, 1983):

> For an investigation on teaching methods to be convincing, it is crucial that the theoretical distinctions between the methods are clearly defined, and can be empirically backed by classroom observation, or by some other technique of documenting the instructional variables.

It is thus especially encouraging to read Margaret Wells' contribution to this volume, which describes an experiment to contrast and compare two methods of teaching grammar in a comprehensive school, over a three-year period, within the context of the National Curriculum. With the principal researcher also being a full-time teacher, there are great hopes that this spotlight on grammar teaching will have most interesting conclusions. It is consequently amply justified that her article should be included here, even though the work is as yet incomplete.

Diana Kent's essay takes us into the realm of teacher training and illustrates how, in Stirling University, habits of reflection are developed through *techniques of micro-teaching recorded on video. This technique involves trainees in a high-risk activity where faults are open to public glare and gawp. It speaks very highly of the tutors that they are able to mediate the recordings in such a way that trainees are assisted in their developing professionalism. The potential of this way of reflecting on one's own teaching is enormous and we can study Diana Kent's contributions with profit.*

Antony Peck's essay shows a different approach to the development of habits of reflection in another training course, considerably shorter and thus more intensive than that at Stirling. This essay studies whether and, if so, how postgraduate student teachers of foreign languages at York's Language Teaching Centre developed habits of reflection. It is done by administering three questionnaires, one in each term of the three-term course, and shows that some of the students studied are likely to become reflective teachers.

We begin, though, with Margaret Wells' school-based study of grammar teaching.

REFLECTING ON GRAMMAR TEACHING
by Margaret Wells

I have focused my research project on an examination of grammar teaching. My decision to research this field has coincided with the advent of the National Curriculum, which in its Final Proposal of October 1990, sections 9.14 to 9.22, made the assumption that a foreign language might be taught through its own medium. Grammar should be taught as an implicit component of the whole subject, and therefore should also be taught in the target language by naturalistic methods, echoing primary practice. I picked up the caveat (9.18) which provided for the use of brief summaries of grammar in English as a means of consolidating learning and decided to employ this as a differentiator in my plan to stage a contrastive study of teaching styles.

A whole year group, the Year 9 intake of 1991, was selected for a three-year longitudinal inquiry for French up to GCSE, after having been divided into two halves, as is usual for the purposes of timetabling. My project became an exploration of:

Implicit grammar teaching	contrasted with	Implicit grammar teaching *plus* Explicit grammar explanations *in English*

Summarised as:

Method *(of teaching grammar)*	contrasted with	Method + ingredient X

Symbols used in this article:

G - I *(I for implicit)*	contrasted with	G - E *(E for explicit)*

The exercise is an anthropological investigation in real terms. I am now at the half-way stage of my classroom-based experiment. The outcomes which I clearly perceive to date fall into categories as follows:

a. benefits to all who participate in the work, including myself, therefore to the department as a whole;

b. problems or disadvantages affecting the project, or affecting the purpose and outlook of the pupils and staff.

Benefits from the research

Taking these considerations in order and beginning, therefore, with a survey of the benefits to the whole department derived from the research so far, I would list the following as major factors:

- CLARIFICATION OF PLACE OF GRAMMAR
  The department has consolidated its approach to classroom practice. The question of the place of grammar in teaching has been clarified, and a plan for grammatical teaching and for the implementation of the target language as the subject medium is underway. It will be monitored at regular intervals.

- COHESION AND EFFICIENCY
  The department may be seen to be functioning more cohesively and more efficiently than before. This is to the benefit of the pupils, of the teachers and, hopefully, of the quality of the learning.

- PREPARATION FOR NATIONAL CURRICULUM
  The department is preparing its ground for the arrival into the 13-18 high

school in September 1994 of the full reality of the National Curriculum for modern languages, as it puts important points of methodology in practice.

- ASSESSMENT AND PROFILING
  The department may be seen to operate an even more closely structured and better co-ordinated system of assessment and profiling than hitherto, from which parents as well as pupils and teachers will benefit.

- CONTRIBUTION TO THE DEBATE
  The department feels that it is making a contribution to the historically protracted debate on methodology in modern languages pedagogy and specifically to the issue of grammar teaching.

- SELF-EVALUATION
  The research focus requires the department's teachers to take an objective look at themselves as practitioners and to assess their own performance, as well as to study the reaction of their pupils more keenly than they would perhaps otherwise do.

- HARD THINKING
  The department's teachers are asked to think seriously and diagnostically about specific methodological approaches to their work instead of having the convenient freedom to use any teaching style they choose, including a variety of soft options.

- CLOSE TEAM WORK
  Due to the intensity of the research work in its practical form, the department's teachers have become involved in close team work which has resulted in greater mutual understanding, and in the sharing of ideas. The whole team accepts that each is responsible and accountable to the others in a real way.

- CLEARER UNDERSTANDING OF PUPILS
  There has developed for teachers a clearer perception of the pupils of the year group in question, from the point of view of their learning processes, of their subject progress, of their conceptual advancement and of their motivation, in line with their personal and physiological development. Teacher-pupil relationships have been magnified:

  a. through the special quality of the project; and
  b. through the intensifying effect of the devices which are employed for the investigation of the attitudes of the participants, e.g. questionnaires, discussions, interviews and case studies.

- PUPIL DEVELOPMENT
  For the first time ever, in our case, we have found ourselves in possession of

the opportunity of taking the same pupils through the three years of their main schooling from Year 9 to their French examination target in Year 11. We are able to observe their psychology and their development from embryo to chrysalis, as it were, and to study the dissembling individual that each pupil of this age group is as he or she occupies a place in each year/phase of the course, apparently as a different individual each time. It seems that we have a better opportunity than ever before to get into the minds of our pupils and observe their conceptual development. We use topics and themes which equate with 'areas of experience'. At this mid-point of the research exercise we have touched on and returned to a number of topics, and we have covered the Perfect tense three times, the Imperfect tense twice, the Future tense twice, Pronouns twice... and so it goes on. We rely on these repeats. It suits our pupils' rate and pattern of development to revisit grammar points, since the process of repetition in the syllabus is a substitute for the genuine type of repetition which eludes the ordinary classroom.

- BENEFIT TO PUPILS
  Where specifically the pupils are concerned, they benefit from the research project by the very reason that it elevates their position in the department. They are very important to the work which is underway and their interests and motivation are taken seriously. They are partners in the work on almost equal terms with the teachers. Negotiation and discussion underpin classroom activity. The pupils are fully stretched by the work and are aware that they are involved in research. For the most part they give it credit for being important and they feel important to it, important in themselves.

Difficulties

The difficulties which, on the other hand, have characterised my research work so far have been as diverse in nature as the benefits. I am grateful that they have been quite emphatically outweighed by the advantages, although they have admittedly been an ever-present reminder of the problematic non-linear nature of a prolonged exercise which is necessarily punctuated by a variety of variables ranging from small, aggravating nuisances through to actual crises which threaten the well-being, perhaps even the further life of the project. Let me explain.

- STRAINS AND TENSIONS
  There is the problem of the strains and tensions imposed on colleagues and pupils co-opted into the experiment. A research leader, who will alone ultimately make off with the final reward, does not enjoy being responsible for the discomfiture of others.

- PUTTING INTO PRACTICE
  There is the problem that, in a research project like my own, the instigator cannot be sure that the team members are indeed fully putting all the agreed

rules of the exercise into practice. The audio recordings of lessons, of teachers' and pupils' discussions, a regular system of questionnaires and opportunities for commenting on business matters have all together provided a checking system. (This checking system in itself affords me the benefit of appraising colleagues' teaching stances and pupils' attitudes to learning.)

Immanent in the situation, however, certain potential irritations have been found lurking. These have at times become realities to frustrate and upset our applecart: items get lost, recordings are accidentally erased, deadlines cannot be met, pupils are absent and sometimes, when group sizes are reduced, comparative assessment is made difficult. When the going gets tough, some weaker pupils see their work as a job relating more to 'Mrs Wells' experiment' rather than to their natural course to GCSE.

- LACK OF AUTONOMY
  A major difficulty arises out of my lack of autonomy. A department is putty in the hands of its school's timetable - and its curriculum manager, for whom it is one thing to mobilise a research project in terms of timetable and staffing for one year, but quite another thing to keep the patterns consistent, and set the exercise up for a second year, not to mention a third! In this, I am talking life and death terms, potentially, for the project. It is difficult to fight battles of this kind when school management has more departments, more staff, more issues to be concerned with than those of one person or of one department area. There is also, of course, the knowledge that a research project might be a matter of passion for its author but evokes no emotion beyond polite interest in other people. This is unfortunate, since it cannot be put into place or conducted without other people's help, agreement or approval. Patient negotiation and some manipulation and manoeuvre play a role in keeping the project afloat.

- RESEARCH DESIGN
  There is a problem also in the research design. The formula for my research may be recalled as Method (Grammar-implicit)=(G-I) versus Method+X (Grammar explicit)=(G-E). The problem for myself and my colleagues lies more and more with the term 'implicit' and with what this means for our work within the research description. Quite simply, we find that we are unable to teach implicitly all the time to our own and our pupils' satisfaction. Some grammar items have defied our attempts to convey them through example and practice, by naturalistic methods based in good primary practice, as the National Curriculum Proposal for Modern Languages (October 1990) would have us do. The Perfect tense alone, possibly also the differentiation of Perfect and Imperfect tenses, could perhaps act as examples of items which have obstructed our progress and our success with the Implicit Method. Of course, other grammar rules are more amenable and better suited to the implicit treatment. For the time being we are relieved to have adjusted our methodological straitjacket slightly. We now count as being

implicit any teaching done wholly in the foreign language, fully explained even, but without the aid of technical jargon and not accompanied by formal notes.

Personal costs and rewards

There have been some costs and rewards for myself personally. Other people's difficulties and worries have been and are mine, all the more because I must be concerned to sustain a good level of motivation for my colleagues and our pupils, and not overburden them in the roles which they play in the scheme of things. By the same token, their rewards and successes are also my own, and they furnish my work with enhancing qualities which will lead, I hope, to good results at each stage of its development and to an interesting outcome ultimately. I look after the welfare of my team and do all I can to ensure that a sense of optimism permeates our camp.

I now know more about grammar teaching that I did beforehand, through the process of conceptualising the Implicit-Explicit approach which defines my research project. Initially, I had taken it for granted that I could perform the Implicit approach. In practice, however, I was taken by surprise by its difficulty and by my own relative incapacity in effecting it. I shall probably never take things for granted about teaching again. I wonder how much I have taken for granted about teaching since I began in 1960? Until now I have never been totally confined to the restrictions of one style, and never so wholly accountable for my performance in it. All of this means, of course, that I have discovered more about myself as a teacher, as a departmental manager and as a person, as my research has proceeded.

Personal outcomes

If there are outcomes in the research done so far, these are perhaps only superficial and certainly they constantly change. At the end of the first year the evidence showed each faction of the experiment in a quite distinctive light, demonstrating quality and quantity respectively as follows:

a. The G-I group were less astute than their G-E counterparts. They explored the foreign language as a means of expressing their ideas and of communicating (exactly as the GCSE would have them do), unhindered by the real complexities of grammar and rather unaware of the existence of these anyway. They were much less adept in formal, structural terms, better intuitively and more productive.

b. The G-E group were grammar-attentive, linguistically cautious, more painstaking than adventurous in their use of French and less successfully productive, however, than the G-I group.

At this mid-point of the second phase of the classroom research, however, there is accumulating evidence to suggest that consolidation of language awareness and linguistic ability is forming for the G-E pupils. The G-I group are at present not able to consolidate their learning in the same way. I am aware that changes will happen all the time as my research exercise develops.

In concluding these reflections I should like to suggest that now is a good time for anyone to mount a longitudinal study, since the potentially disrupting option factor has been removed from the scene and replaced by the principle of a 'foreign language for all'. Moreover, the in-situ practitioner may feel encouraged to do naturalistic research, confident that he or she can obtain a really relevant set of data. As has already been seen, any research venture will be beset with problems and obstacles, but motivation, imagination and flexibility can sustain it. The plan with which the researcher sets out changes all the time, even though the focus remains constant, due to the characters, ideas and ideals which animate the project, and due to the needs and necessities which arise. There can, of course, in any case be no straightforward performance when the cast of players is composed of some teachers and many children, all of whom are different, unpredictable, perhaps unreliable, possibly inconstant and certainly inconsistent.

The very unpredictability of the outcomes to which I allude here is the element of my research which excites me the most and which keeps my task fresh. So, with the conclusion to my research project still so far away, I can only rely on the variety of experience accumulated so far to sustain me across the terrain still to be covered and on to further reflections.

While Margaret Wells is concerned with a finely focused study of implicit and explicit grammar teaching methods, producing valuable reflections on her own and her colleagues' practice at every step, Diana Kent portrays for us a process no less valuable in its consequences for the participants. To teach in front of a video camera takes courage. Many people are showing this bravery as Diana Kent and others treading the same dangerous path show.

THE FOUNDATIONS OF A REFLECTIVE TEACHER
by Diana Kent

This article will describe one model of developing the reflective teacher. It is a product of dissatisfaction with my own experience of traditional teacher training methods and the conviction that a better way must be possible.

I am particularly fortunate in having the opportunity of working in Stirling University which, throughout its 25 years of existence, has given teacher education a high profile. The Stirling structure lends itself particularly well to the development of reflective practitioners. It is a concurrent course which prepares teachers of French, Spanish and German for the secondary system. Students study in the language departments and simultaneously complete a degree and diploma in Education. Professional training in specific curricular areas does not commence until the fourth semester of a course which will, in total, consist of nine semesters in the University and, in addition, a year spent working abroad as a language assistant in a secondary school. Throughout this time the student will undertake some 22 weeks of practical school experience and sixteen exposures to micro-teaching.

What a reflective teacher does

In saying that this particular structure is propitious for the development of a reflective practitioner, I am making certain assumptions about the nature of a reflective teacher. The reflective teacher is one who is capable of self-criticism. She thinks about the effectiveness of her teaching and is able to evaluate her effectiveness in the process of assisting good quality learning. She will be capable of adjusting her strategies to suit context, objective and learner and, in the event of an unsatisfactory outcome, she will adapt her method and strategies appropriately. The reflection consists of comparing the real outcome with an ideal or desired outcome. Any recognised deficit between real and ideal constitutes a problem for the practitioner. Both the recognition of the problem, and the attempt to find a solution to it, are features of a reflective practitioner.

Practical theory

Developing such a teacher is not just a matter of imparting knowledge and technique mixed together in equal proportions. Fundamental to reflection is a teacher's 'practical theory'. For a definition of 'practical theory' I use that of Handal and Lauvas (1987):

> ... 'practical theory' refers to a person's private, integrated but ever changing system of knowledge, experience and values which is relevant to teaching practice at any particular time.

Most students begin professional development with a highly developed 'practical theory' of teaching. The theory may not be a conscious theory but its influence on teaching performance will be nonetheless powerful. It is part of the business of teacher education to bring to the surface of consciousness this 'baggage' of practical theory and thus give the student the opportunity to question its reliability. In this way the student becomes consciously responsible for her own 'practical theory'. Where it is found wanting, the process of teacher education should aim to assist the future teacher to develop a more reliable theory founded on relevant knowledge and wider experience. It is not the responsibility of the teacher trainer to provide the student with an alternative practical theory but to enable her to constantly reconstruct her theory in the light of new experience and knowledge. This should involve her in a lifetime cycle of application, observation, evaluation and adaptation. It is this ability to constantly reconstruct theory which differentiates the reflective from the non-reflective teacher.

Micro-teaching

The first stage of this development process, that is the surfacing of the incipient trainee's practical theory, depends on the use of micro-teaching. Micro-teaching allows every student a weekly half-hour lesson with a reduced number of school pupils from either Primary 7 or Secondary 1 and consists of two phases, each of eight weeks. The function of the first four lessons of the first phase of micro-teaching, from the professional point of view, is to get the student to reveal her practical theory.

This can only be achieved by the student doing the teaching with as little interference as possible. This 'doing' will then become the focus of analysis by means of review and discussion with both peers and tutor. In order to avoid interference, almost no advice is proffered by the tutor. For the actual lessons students are given clear objectives for both pupils and students but almost no direction as to strategies to be employed. This causes some distress in a minority of students who, misreading the situation, feel that they are being treated negligently by their tutor in not being given step-by-step instructions! For the majority a realisation of the tutor's purpose has dawned when the time comes to complete the end-of-semester course evaluation forms (fortunately for the tutor), but there is always someone who has, despite explanation, failed to appreciate the purpose of the exercise.

The exercise brings to light very interesting performance features which yield valuable insights into the unconscious beliefs about how a teacher operates. Very often these are a throwback to quite recent experience as a school pupil. It must be borne in mind that the typical Scottish student at Stirling will only have left school some two and a half years earlier and will probably be only 20 years old. Other students consciously or unconsciously imitate the behaviour of the teaching which they are currently experiencing in the languages departments of the University. In either case, the method used is not geared or adapted to the specific requirements of the micro-teaching context. Not all students show this pattern of regression: there are always some who are already aware, or who quickly become aware of their practical theory and who consequently adapt or refine it to suit the new situation better.

Post-lesson review

Reviewing of the video recording both by peer group and by the tutor is the linchpin of this process. Of course, for the institution, it is costly both in time and attention. Through this process of consultation the student becomes aware of the hypotheses or premises which form part of her initial practical theory. This awareness brings with it a realisation of the possibility and, in many cases, the necessity for developing or actualising the theory through increased knowledge and experience. It constitutes the foundation of the future teacher's education. The entire process can be seen as a stocktaking exercise for both the student and the tutor; it serves to establish a point of departure for a joint collaboration in development.

Seminars

Simultaneously with the micro-teaching, the student is attending seminars which provide a terminology which will assist her to analyse and talk about the practical theory revealed in her own performance in the micro-teaching lessons. The seminars also serve to expand the student's knowledge in the area of learning theory, more specifically language learning theory, applied linguistics and the rise of technology. Students are asked to consider the interrelationship of these factors in the evolution of methodology over the last century. The content of these courses expands the knowledge of the future teacher but, more importantly, it helps her to realise that no definitive 'best way' of learning and teaching languages has yet been established. This should, theoretically, bring home the message that each teacher is, to some extent, responsible for the push forward towards a better way. It should also protect the student against forces or fashions which try to indoctrinate one particular 'correct' method.

Risk-taking and experimentation

The second four sessions of micro-teaching encourage the student teacher to experiment in converting the new knowledge, gained in the seminars, into classroom practice. Risk-taking and experimentation are encouraged as the micro-teaching is not part of the grading system. All the time the student is developing, through consultation with the peer group and in review of the recordings with the tutor, a capacity for objective observation and evaluation of achievement. This is, perhaps, the most valuable aspect of this phase of developing the reflective practitioner. In this way expanding knowledge and experience integrate in the conscious refinement of the practical theory. There is an on-going cyclical interaction between received knowledge and experiential knowledge and each of these, in turn, both affects practice and is affected by practice. The 'doing' and the thinking about the 'doing' are constantly interrelated.

The student spends the following year working as a foreign language assistant in the country of her first foreign language. This year abroad gives her time to digest the experience of the earlier semester and at the same time provides valuable new experience in the classroom which will enrich her practical theory. As she will be teaching her mother tongue, she is relieved of the separate stress of 'correct language' and can focus on professional aspects.

The following semester continues the process of integrating the knowledge and experience which form the basis of the student-teacher's practical theory. Micro-teaching continues to play an important role in the integration process but emphasis shifts from establishing the initial audit of the student's 'baggage' to the widening of experience and experimentation with strategies. Most students have, by this time, developed an adequate expertise in observation and self-criticism. Clearly the group will not be homogeneous but, given the individual attention offered to each student, it is possible to address individual needs.

Concurrent nature of 'doing' and 'reflecting'

It is not my concern in this brief article to describe the entire content of the course, merely to point out the effort to encourage reflection in the future practitioner. The indispensable characteristic of this system is the concurrent nature of 'doing' and reflecting. Essential, too, is the consciousness of one's practical theory and the recognition that it should be a theory constantly subjected to testing and refinement throughout one's working life. This is not a comfortable model for the future teacher. It would be much more comforting to be able to offer a formula which would last for life. Equally so for the teacher trainer - it would be so much simpler to create a package of training materials which promise a panacea for every occasion: a package which could be delivered without the time-consuming consultation process and would be very economical for the institution and for the relevant authority. However, it comes back to a matter of belief and if we believe in the value of the reflective teacher, then there seems to be little possibility of short cuts for any of those involved in the process.

We now follow a group of trainees on a one-year, intensive post-graduate training course, as they are encouraged to put down on paper their thoughts about reflection, and any effects it had as they progressed through their training. Antony Peck also asks whether trainees' habits of reflection develop in a noticeable way as the course proceeds.

Just as research into language teaching and learning has, over the last five or six years, assumed an increasing importance, so, during the same period, the developing expertise of teachers in training has attracted attention. The initial training of teachers (HMI, 1987) and what used to be the probationary year (HMI, 1988) were closely examined, and the establishment of the Council for the Accreditation of Teacher Education (CATE) focused public awareness on the content and method of training, as well as the competencies required by classroom teachers. As everyone is aware, the process is on-going.

REFLECTION AS AN AID TO SELF-IMPROVEMENT
by Antony Peck

The need to reflect

It is above all the isolation of the teacher in his or her classroom for virtually the whole of a professional career, with little opportunity to observe and learn from colleagues, that provides much of the current impetus for research into language classrooms. Theories of language teaching and learning have affected, some would say infected, the profession since language teaching began. Teachers approach them rightly with some scepticism. But the desirability of reflecting calmly on one's teaching is unquestioned.

What is reflection? Calderhead (1989) sees the teaching which arises from mature reflection as being 'intelligent action, in which its justification and consequences had been considered'. He follows Dewey (1933), for whom the concept meant 'active, persistent and careful consideration of any belief or supposed form of knowledge in the light of the grounds that support it and the further conclusions to which it tends'. Reflection is the final stage of the perpetually renewed cycle which begins with planning, continues with self-awareness and self-observation, and concludes with self-evaluation. Looking back to the classroom events of a completed lesson or cycle of lessons is the necessary basis for subsequent planning and teaching. It is, as researchers into teacher training perceive (Livingstone and Borko, 1989), an element of teaching vital to include in training, since 'the opportunity to repeat and fine-tune instructional strategies and explanations increases the likelihood that novices will incorporate these elements into their cognitive schemata'. This view is supported by Alexander and his colleagues (Alexander, Muir and Chant, 1992) who 'view both perspective and interpretation as essential component skills in the acquisition of general teaching capability because they are fundamental to the teacher's professional day'.

It is not only necessary for a teacher to reflect, in order to plan ahead; it is also necessary to learn how to reflect. Teachers in training are often poor judges of their teaching performance, as a tutor's invitation to a trainee to comment on a lesson just completed frequently demonstrates. Calderhead (Calderhead and Robson, 1991) finds that novices' understanding of their classroom practice is rather scant, whereas 'the knowledge of the expert or experienced teacher... is more systematically organised and related to specific classroom contexts'.

The scope of this study

During the year 91/92, eight of the 83 modern linguists being trained at the Language Teaching Centre at York University were invited to take part in a survey, requiring them to respond to three questionnaires, one during each term. Seven of the eight had taken a UK first degree in a modern language or languages; the eighth was a native speaker of German with a *Staatsexamen* in Theology. Their course lasted 36 weeks and consisted of observation in a primary school, lectures and discussions on issues affecting all teachers, and an intensive programme focused on the didactics and pedagogy of foreign language teaching, supported by substantial school experience and a thirteen-week block of teaching practice.

The linguists had a programme of study which was to a great extent standardised. Only one element of the programme, lesson planning, dealt specifically with the need to reflect on lessons, and the course required such self-appraisal to figure, in writing, on lesson plans for inspection by tutors. However, it is likely that students would have picked up from the rich programme of inputs into their PGCE course, not least from teachers in school, an awareness that they should continually evaluate their own practice, with a view to improving their teaching performance.

The research focus

It is most unlikely that the need to establish habits of reflection protruded as a more salient feature of the course than others for the majority of students. It may have loomed somewhat larger for the group of nine correspondents, though there is no means of quantifying this. The questionnaires attempted to find out through a variety of questions how students' habits of reflection were formed, and concentrated on the following enquiries.

1. Do you think carefully about your teaching?
2. Which aspect of your language teaching do you reflect on most?
3. How do you organise your self-evaluation?
4. Have you noticed any improvements?

A more implicit question was planted in the longitudinal study, namely, do these trainees reflect in a more systematic or sophisticated way at the end of their course than they did at the beginning? This is to ask a similar question to that posed by Russell (Russell and Munby, 1991), namely, did these students learn by and from experience, so that the 'frame' which constrains the scope of their self-awareness can be seen to change throughout the 36 weeks of their training? Were there any signs of the eight becoming reflective teachers (Winitzky, 1992) in the sense that they systematically analysed their own teaching and tried to understand why particular teaching actions have particular effects with a given group of students?

The first questionnaire

This was issued three weeks before the end of the autumn term, when the trainees had observed professional language teachers at work on a number of occasions, and had themselves contributed parts of lessons under the direction of a teacher or a tutor. Their block teaching practice was to start at the beginning of the following term.

The first inquiry sought to establish whether or not the students in training already perceived that areas of their developing expertise were likely to need improvement. Of the eight, four were unable at this stage to identify any such aspect. Among the responses of the remainder, most were concerned about their ability to plan lessons which would be interesting and contain a variety of techniques. Other areas already identified for improvement by at least two trainees were *'preparing lessons which differentiate for different levels of ability within the classroom'*, *'giving clear and explicit instructions'* for activities such as pair and group work, and *'building cross-curricular issues into my teaching'*.

Other concerns were to do with pitching lessons correctly: *'progressing through presentation and practice in small steps rather than jumping ahead and expecting too much too soon'*, classroom management: *'getting attention immediately'*, using their subsidiary foreign language, and introducing IT.

Trainees were also asked if they had heard of, or encountered any ways of thinking about their teaching with a view to improving it. While all the respondents said they had met such ways, two misunderstood the question, naming techniques they thought would be most likely to promote and maintain such improvement: *'keeping tasks varied, change-overs well organised, voice levels audible, and blackboard presentation clear'*.

Other methods of reflection, each mentioned twice, were *'to assess and reassess'* all aspects of one's teaching, and to *'think about methodology'*; to ask a colleague to *'observe lessons and give constructive criticism'*; and to *'ask pupils to complete questionnaires about the effectiveness of lessons'*. This last procedure was however seen to *'be most controversial and difficult to introduce'*. The following statement summed up perhaps the degree to which the group felt at this stage to be prepared for some form of reflection on their own teaching.

'*I still haven't really experienced classroom teaching on my own, and I can't really say how I'll assess it effectively. I'll try anything to start with! I would like to think that my instincts will tell me where I'm going wrong, but I will appreciate the help of staff.*'

The questionnaire also asked respondents to speculate on which human or technical resources they expected to be available to help them during their teaching practice term. No doubt can exist that novice teachers need and expect to receive sympathetic and helpful advice through a variety of formal and informal discussions with other people, such as teacher colleagues, their tutor, and friends from whom they expect to receive support and advice. While all students expect to find the '*enthusiastic and supportive mentor*' being the model, the majority also expect to find physical resources available to them '*in the staff library*' in the form of textbooks, '*up-to-date reports and publications on teaching in general and modern languages in particular*'. Some students look to other trainees, themselves on teaching practice, as a resource in the search for effectiveness, envisaging '*peer assessment during team-teaching sessions*', while others seek '*the opportunity to video a lesson and review it later*'. Three respondents saw pupils as a resource aiding reflection, one seeing '*a readiness within myself to react positively to reactions of the pupils*'.

Summary

The first third of the PGCE training course finds these students relatively unaware of those aspects of their teaching most likely to need improvement, with the exception of planning. They were also unclear about how to implement any conscious programme of reflection, though they saw clearly the need for supportive, sympathetic and systematic advice from others, more experienced than themselves.

The second questionnaire

This was issued near the end of the teaching practice term and only succeeded in eliciting responses from five of the original nine respondents. It sought to establish which aspect of their teaching had required the greatest effort from students to raise to their desired standards, and which conscious changes had been made in order to bring about improvements.

Within the strict area of foreign language teaching it was lesson planning and preparation that the majority found most taxing.
'*I put a lot of effort into devising lessons and producing materials, which would provide clear and stimulating presentation and maximum opportunity for all pupils to practice.*'

Maintaining classroom discipline was also seen as a major problem for three of the respondents. One consciously '*stepped up*' threats and incentives in an attempt to obtain satisfactory behaviour, a move prompted by *'a really wild lesson with my tutor group and rather severe criticism from a teacher observing'*. One student teacher found it necessary to radically alter the way instructions were given before starting an activity.

> *'I realised you can never go slow enough, or repeat instructions too often.'* This was a realisation that followed *'activities that fell apart due to insufficient instruction'*.

Another trainee had to attend to *'differentiation and pitching the lesson to various (pupils') abilities'*, necessitated because *'some pupils were not coping, while others had finished and were wasting time'*.

Another became *'less bound by the textbook'*, showing *'more willingness to venture (away) from the topics and language covered by the book'*, a course of action initiated when it was *'realised that some improvisation and variation was beneficial and enjoyable to the students'*.

The questionnaire attempted also to find out which techniques of reflection were most used by the student teachers, which were estimated by them to have been of the greatest significance, and on which they placed greatest reliance.

All the students said they relied on the comments of their tutor as a means of reflecting on their teaching. More important still, however, were discussions held with fellow PGCE students, as were the comments given by the class teacher. These ranked, along with the observations of another teacher, as the most significant means of reflecting.

Among other techniques singled out for mention were the annotation of lesson plans on completion of the lesson, the immediate design of the next lesson plan for the same class, discussions with friends not concerned with foreign language teaching, inquiry amongst pupils, reference to notes made during the autumn term at the university, and the use of feedback from tests.

Correspondents were given a list of nine aspects of their teaching which might be expected to change and develop over the period of teaching practice. In order to determine whether they were conscious of any such changes, they were invited to tick items accordingly, add further ones if they wished, and make comments.

All the students reported that they had changed the way they managed and controlled the class.

> *'I rearranged desks for their lessons and concentrated on those types of activities they seemed to respond to most positively.'*
> *'I increased the amount of walking about; and separated trouble-makers more often.'*
> *'I became more confident, especially when I knew their names. I was less frightened to move chatterers.'*

The trainees also reported changes to their way of planning lessons.

> '*I took less time; I didn't plan so far in advance, i.e. I came down from two weeks to two days.*'
>
> '*I actually planned what I was going to say in the foreign language.*'

These were the major changes reported but, additionally, a majority referred to changing their objectives for a given class.

> '*For a very low ability Year 8 class, I restricted my language objectives and reduced the amount of writing.*'

Changes in the use of language learning activities were also reported.

> '*I used more group-oriented activities in the second half.*'
>
> '*As time went on, I saw the value of using some traditional grammatical exercises with some groups.*'

The ways in which trainees made their teaching intentions clear and unambiguous to the class were also subject to change.

> '*I checked their understanding of instructions in English and had the students repeat them to each other.*'

Asked how their own image of themselves as a teacher had changed during the period, all students responded. Here are some verbatim remarks.

> '*I felt more at ease towards the end and was therefore able to enjoy the experience much more. **But** some ideals had to be accepted as impossible, e.g. 100% use of target language.*'
>
> '*I have to be more forceful and stricter in the classroom.*'
>
> '*I'd always been very relaxed and familiar with my classes. However, in a secondary school situation this is not immediately appropriate, and I found I had to become stricter and more formal in my approach.*'
>
> '*I feel more confident in myself and in my teaching ability. This was reinforced by other teachers' comments, pupils' reactions and comments at a parents' evening.*'
>
> '*I became aware of the need not to save on time for self-reflection, and to make constant efforts to reflect.*'

Summary

At the end of the thirteen weeks' teaching practice, significant changes are apparent in these students' approach to reflection. They were clear about their strengths and weaknesses, and what required the greatest effort to improve. They had used a wide variety of reflection techniques and, in surveying their own development throughout the term, they noted changes in many areas of their experience, which they referred to in concrete terms, sometimes very vividly.

The third questionnaire

The purpose of the third questionnaire, completed at the end of the PGCE year, was to find out whether habits of reflection had been sufficiently well established to remain vividly in trainees' memory, and whether they were likely to be used once professional life had begun. Correspondents' advice was sought, also, about how best to anchor reflection techniques in the training course content for the future.

Since the questionnaires were anonymous, no individual students' development could be traced. It was clear, however, that the means of reflecting on one's teaching remained clearly in the memory of this group, virtually all those techniques mentioned previously recurring. It was the notation of plans after a lesson, the one specific technique advocated at the university in the autumn term, which was the most frequently mentioned.

> *'Notes following a lesson, and listing possible improvements and alternatives for next time.'*
> *'Carefully reading over the plan after the lesson. Noting down observations.'*
> *'Looking at lesson plans; comparing them with reality.'*

The questionnaire also showed that a general need in professional life for reflection on one's own practice was recognised (though one correspondent felt less likely to assess whether lesson objectives had been met), some trainees being ruefully aware that the opportunities to discuss lessons with fellow students and colleagues would be far less.

Everyone felt that reflection should be given considerable emphasis throughout the PGCE course, and a number of specific recommendations were made. One student hoped that opportunities for reciprocal observation by pairs of trainees during teaching practice would be made generally available: *'I think having a fellow student observing lessons should be encouraged...'*. Another advocated that reflection should automatically trigger interventionist action: *'...how to go about putting information gleaned from reflection into practical improvements...'*. Two trainees wanted the course to provide them with specific lesson descriptors, or competencies, with which they could *'analyse the 'success' of a lesson'*. Examples included: *'questions one should ask oneself, e.g. Did I involve all class members? Did my chosen activities match my chosen goals?'*.

Summary

At the end of the PGCE course, it seemed that awareness of the need to reflect on one's teaching was well-established; certainly these students wanted increased emphasis on it for their successors.

Students' type of reflection

It is interesting to note that by the end of the PGCE year, this admittedly small group of students had shown that they knew and accepted that they would be self-reliant when evaluating their own teaching, even though they advocated stronger and clearer guidance from the university for their successors. They did not appear to fall into Korthagen's (1988) categories of students either with an internal orientation, viewing learning to teach as a voyage of self-discovery, or with an external orientation, relying mostly on tutorial guidance.

The language of reflection

The replies to the first questionnaire, before teaching practice, followed Calderhead's expectations (1989) in that little ability to analyse their forthcoming teaching appeared to be in place, with four students unable to identify any aspect of their teaching likely to require special attention, while those who did expressed themselves mostly in general terms. By contrast, the language and observations of the second questionnaire, after teaching practice, were more precise, concrete, and sometimes colourful. The third questionnaire, though containing only one question capable of eliciting information relevant to students' own ideas about techniques of reflection, hinted nevertheless at nascent criteria for the evaluation of their own teaching.

Final summary

No claim is made for any statistical significance of the findings of this survey, since the sample was tiny. There are signs, nonetheless, that the PGCE course can develop habits of reflective teaching.

This chapter has much that ought to be reassuring for language teachers. It shows that certain ideas, deeply implanted in various aspects of our personal life, endure from one generation to another. Language teaching has always been peculiarly subject to swings of opinion, bandwagons and gimmicks, but this chapter draws our attention to ancient concerns being presented in a fresh light.

Teaching grammar is still on the agenda. How could it be otherwise? Let us hope that Margaret Wells' work will give a new impetus to this central element of our work, and keep it firmly in our sights. No-one can produce a new, original sentence without a knowledge of grammatical structure, so grammar teaching is at the heart of our professionalism.

Teaching specific things to small groups as a way of learning one's craft also has an excellent pedigree. It is the equivalent of going in at the shallow end. Diana Kent shows how this well-used technique, by which the teaching situation can be to some extent controlled so that the trainee can experiment and make mistakes before being let loose in a school, makes use of video technology at Stirling University. It is, thus, both old and new.

The York survey of how post-graduate trainees developed patterns of reflection during their training course indicates that the oldest truth of all - that one must depend on oneself for improvement - is still under active and enthusiastic consideration.

Here, then, are three traditional concerns of language teaching, each in an up-to-date context.

Plus ça change...

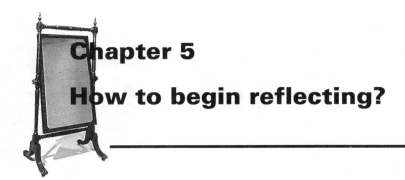

Chapter 5

How to begin reflecting?

By now it will be evident that teachers who reflect in any systematic way upon what goes on in their classrooms have to develop the skills which such activity requires. The skills of reflection, like any others, improve with practice and, sometimes, with a bit of help. They can also benefit, as Chris Kyriacou has earlier suggested, from a supportive environment.

Teachers in today's schools may of course need less convincing of the many benefits associated with successful reflection than of the possibility of making a start - which is the subject of this final chapter. Given the pressure of work currently being carried by most teachers, as well as the traditional isolation behind a closed classroom door still experienced by many, the most helpful questions for us to address will be:

• What user-friendly ways are there of 'putting a toe in the water'?

and

• How can teachers of modern languages be helped on their way towards a reflective mode of practice?

It goes without saying that teachers are perfectly capable of expanding their skills and expertise. Moreover, when carrying out a classroom inquiry on their own account, rather than just continuing to respond to the myriad of everyday demands made by others, teachers often reveal an astonishing level of enthusiasm, for example speaking of their investigations in terms of 'the only thing that keeps me sane' or 'my life-line'. The intriguing question remains: how did they begin?

Small-scale semi-private start

Some will feel safest making a small-scale, semi-private start. For them, diary keeping could be a way in. As the Palmers have suggested in Chapter 3, diaries can be most revealing about what is going on under the surface - especially when teacher and pupil thoughts are set alongside each other. A teacher's diary by itself, however, becomes a powerful way of focusing thoughts and feelings, or of helping a teacher to make connections between events and ideas which might otherwise be missed.

Audio cassettes

The simplest device of all for the beginner to use is the audio cassette recorder. Subsequent study of recordings can be conducted in private and may be immensely revealing. Some minor technical matters have all the same to be considered. Since microphones cannot clearly record more than one person talking at once, they have to be somewhat selectively directed, e.g. at the teacher (relatively easy to record) or at a small group of pupils (less easy). In either case, pupils will need at least some brief and reassuring explanation, but they will quickly accept and get used to the presence of a recorder. Some experimentation is nearly always required, however, in obtaining a satisfactory level of recording quality. Criteria for what is 'satisfactory' need be no more than strictly functional: i.e. sufficient for deciphering most of what was said by the speaker(s) targeted.

Useful hints for beginners include: placing something sound-absorbent (e.g. a bit of cloth, the size and thickness of a bathroom flannel) under a recorder with built-in microphone, to cut out motor or other noise which can be magnified by a shiny surface like a desk; keeping any separate microphone close to, and pointing at, its target; a microphone can similarly benefit from a sound-absorbent mat, also from a low L-shaped screen of, say, corrugated cardboard - each wing about A4 size - placed between the back of the microphone and other potential noise. Such devices may improve recordings of pairs or groups, for instance.

Co-operation

There is some evidence to suggest that for some teachers an element of co-operation may play a valuable role in making a start. In the sections which follow, words such as collaboration, networks, or critical friend illustrate this key feature; so do many of the post-course evaluative statements from the Newcastle teachers cited later. A link-up with another teacher or group can make all the difference. Collaboration can be more fun; but obligation to a colleague can also keep one up to the mark of course!

Eryl Griffiths, in her contribution in Chapter 3, has also quoted comments illustrating the same point in relation to peer observation. Sharing is often in itself the source of genuine pleasure and reassurance, as well as of mutual trust; and trust is an indispensable pre-condition for that open-mindedness and risk of self-revelation which many forms of co-operative reflection involve.

Outside support

Some help from outside can also be helpful in prompting and enabling reflection, e.g. a course at a local institution of higher education, or a small-scale inquiry sponsored within a school or a group of schools. The latter possibility, especially, raises issues about attitudes of school management and about a school ethos in which reflection upon practice will be valued and attract its share of resources. That kind of ethos can only develop gradually. It cannot be imposed, and its first stirrings usually require encouragement. It is, nevertheless, often through the initial example of an individual or small group that the seeds of wider developments are sown. Support in the form of advice might be obtained by contacting CILT (and its associated Comenius Centres) or the Scottish CILT.

In-service support varies in the degree of initial commitment it demands. We begin with a brief account, by Antony Peck, of the scope which even very short courses can offer.

THE SHORT OPTION
by Antony Peck

What better way to start reflecting than to observe how others teach? What is more likely to provoke us into experimentation? What is more hopeful of producing new ideas?

Teachers are often isolated in their classrooms. No-one is quite sure how colleagues teach. The National Curriculum requires all pupils to learn a foreign language over five years, and teachers to teach through the medium of the target language. New objectives need new methods.

Our subject is beset with imperatives. It abounds with 'shoulds' and 'oughts' which devalue, disturb and de-skill teachers. Yet such directives have virtually no empirical base derived from classroom research into what actually happens in classrooms.

School-based INSET

One remedy for the above problem is to seek a new type of in-service training (INSET): school-based INSET. Let the schools set the agenda. Let the approach come from an individual languages department. Let languages departments from neighbouring schools make a joint approach.

What might such an approach look like?

- We wish to improve this area of our teaching.
- We want support, and a constructive view from outside, concerning this problem.
- OFSTED is coming; we want a non-judgmental, constructive review of our performance in this area of our work.
- OFSTED has been; how can we implement its proposals?

What role might the provider of a new type of INSET have? It would not provide ready-made solutions. It would not lay down the law. It would not implement top-down treatment. It would help define problems and remedies. It would help departments learn from others with similar needs. It would stimulate reflection and measure effectiveness.

What might the experience be like? Courses of action recommended to departments might include:

- sharing problems and difficulties in a non-threatening manner;
- reciprocal self-help;
- efficient and effective reflection on one's own practice;
- structured observation of other foreign language teachers.

This sort of INSET requires specific techniques for focusing on given aspects of teaching, for monitoring progress, for measuring advances, and for providing after-care.

Who might provide INSET like this? As the balance in the initial training of teachers shifts towards the schools, here is a role for the institutions of higher education.

A longer-term initiative may involve an individual or a small group of colleagues seeking to join a course at a local HE institution or an established action research network. A taught course may also provide the professional contacts from which a network can grow. Quite typically, as explained below, in-service courses are now modular in structure. As such, they can either provide a complete framework within which teachers may reflect upon their own circumstances or practice, or they can offer partial support (e.g. with appropriate inquiry techniques) for teachers wishing to undertake action research. In this section David Westgate describes developments in available support, taking his own department, the School of Education at Newcastle-upon-Tyne, as an example.

GAINING SUPPORT FROM LOCAL HE
by David Westgate

It may be helpful to begin by clarifying some of the consequences of recent changes in in-service courses and their funding. Although fewer secondments are now available, and LEAs offer less funding support, the scope for individual inquiry has in many aspects actually increased (see e.g. Russell and Munby, 1992) - so long as such inquiry is classroom-focused and leads to relatively practical outcomes. This fact should encourage the would-be reflective practitioner, whose inquiries are by their nature more likely to attract financial support from school management than traditional-style courses ever did.

Modules and short courses

Recent changes have also had the effect of passing to schools much of the initiative for defining the kind of support they require. Also, many university education departments (UDEs) have begun to offer a more flexible and user-friendly kind of professional study. Many have, in the jargon, 'modularised' their course. The study unit has typically become the single term, and many UDEs now offer a great variety of course patterns. These include the short and highly specific, as well as others in which an equivalent time is spaced in such ways as to encourage teacher reflection, e.g. the 'four-day' pattern: three consecutive days on release, leading to individually defined school-based projects which are reported on and discussed at the fourth day a month or two later. Some short courses are, by negotiation, conceived as school or consortia events, taking place in the schools themselves or in teacher centres as well as UDEs. Then, too, units can be chained together, as required, into individually tailored courses of study leading to awards, e.g. at diploma or masters degree level.

Small-scale action research

Many such courses are now assessed through assigned work which offers the possibility of individual, small-scale action research, supported not just by the content of the module concerned but also by built-in help with appropriate data-gathering techniques. This kind of assignment brief may prescribe, for example, a course file, consisting of an analysis of issues from course and/or project, related inquiry findings, responses to reading and a 'learning log'; also, an instruction to... 'identify an issue in your current context which requires further investigation, analysing approaches you have adopted to deal with this issue in relation to the experiences developed during the course' and including 'planning, implementation and evaluation' work done up to the point of writing.

In a particularly promising development, it is now possible for assignment topics, even on award-bearing courses, to be co-ordinated in such a way that groups of teachers can feed insights back into the schools (or consortia) where the work has been carried out, for immediate implementation and for other reflective teachers to build on.

An example of an 'integrated modular' programme is given in the diagram overleaf. It represents the pattern of support available at just one UDE, at the University of Newcastle-upon-Tyne, and shows especially the flexibility of courses offered. Responsibility for creating coherence among units chosen has passed to the student. Some combinations of units form natural 'pathways', e.g. where all units fall within one area of study such as classroom language. Other links depend more on individuals' experience or interests.

Continuing development for responsible professionals

A programme like this also demonstrates the extent to which 'reflection on practice' and the needs of the 'reflective practitioner' have become key concepts underlying in-service support. This has moved on from a top-down notion of training towards continuing development for responsible professionals (CPD). Such a structure combines support with an increased potential for teachers themselves to define and control their own reflection agenda and their style of work.

The structure presented through this diagram is of course a general one, showing what is available to teachers of any phase of schooling or any subject. Units in modern foreign languages are identified through the programme brochure. A recent example of an LEA-sponsored four-day MFL course has been entitled 'Providing modern foreign languages across the whole ability range'; it was tutored jointly by MFL and Special Needs specialists. It led to a wide range of classroom-based inquiries and to an important sharing of insights on the final day. 'Current issues in the teaching of MFL' figures in the programme of term-long units; and several teachers (investigating aspects of e.g. grammar teaching, assessment and self-instruction) are registered for higher degrees by thesis. A number of others following taught courses are working on, or have just finished, dissertations on MFL topics.

Figure 5

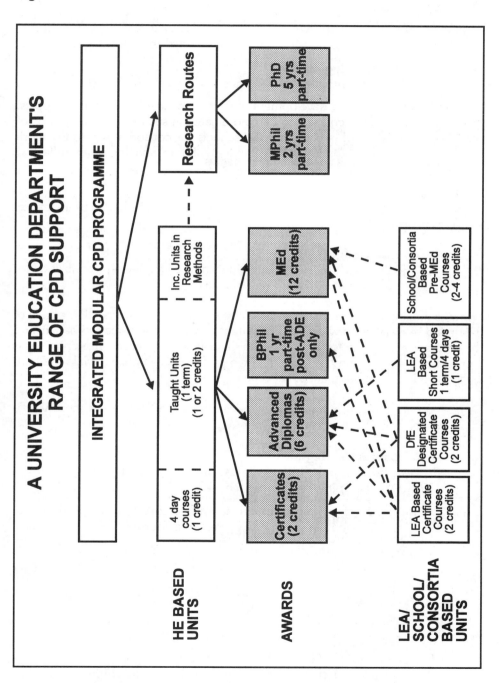

Benefits felt by participating teachers

An analysis of post-course evaluations returned over the past two years reveals numerous benefits felt by participating teachers. They can be grouped as follows:

- **social contact/collegiality**
  involving e.g. opportunities to meet and discuss with others, sharing views, problems, etc.

- **intellectual stimulation**
  involving e.g. rekindled professional interest/sense of purpose, clarified aims, review of effectiveness or teaching strategies

- **personal growth**
  in e.g. self-awareness/self-confidence/self-esteem, and objectivity in respect of own practice

- **research knowledge/skill**
  for e.g. getting back to study, updating knowledge; seeing possibilities for own classroom inquiries, how to gather data

What is striking is the prominence given by these teachers to meeting others of like mind; equally so, however, is the extent to which the perceived benefits go beyond social contact for its own sake. The first and second headings stress content and skills within the teachers' own professional contexts, while the third suggests a lot of commitment to reflection.

A few examples of the phrases used convey these teachers' views more vividly than the above list by itself can do. What they wrote included:

under **social contact/collegiality**
> *'It was a good opportunity to discuss and compare ideas.'*
> *'...hearing the opinions of other teachers.'*

under **intellectual stimulation**
> *'...provided a real jolt to my thinking.'*
> *'It gave me some useful ideas to put into practice immediately.'*
> *'It was a time for reflection, transcending the day-to-day nature of teaching.'*
> *'...developing strategies for assessing how effective the department is.'*
> *'...new perspectives on old problems.'*

under **personal growth**
> *'It gave me the confidence to go back and have a go.'*
> *'...provided me with the insight and self-esteem to continue... and to*

re-discover my vocation.'
'The experience gave me greater knowledge of myself.'
'It has made me look at my role in school in a more detached, less subjective way.'
'...made me much more self-critical.'

under **research knowledge/skill**

'It got me back into the academic literature.'
'...appreciating the possibilities of classroom research.'
'...to be made to collect data that I had been meaning to do for ages.'

These examples do seem to confirm the value which may be placed by teachers upon some formal support as they enter into or sustain a reflective practitioner's role.

They also seem to bear out at least three of the four 'essential characteristics' of reflective teaching which Chris Kyriacou cites in Chapter 1, namely:

- *concern with aims and consequences;*
- *open-mindedness;*
- *self-reflection.*

One could add another:

- *to do with persistence, carrying reflection beyond the initial impetus which gave rise to it and thence back into practice.*

In the next section, Mike Calvert comments upon the experience of encouraging teachers from various LEAs to undertake reflection in the form of small-scale action research. The cyclical notion of such activity is again emphasised, so that his contribution not only relates personal experience but also serves to summarise themes stressed throughout this book - in particular, that of 'reflective practice' as an on-going state of mind for those who get hooked on it!

ACTION RESEARCH: A VEHICLE FOR REFLECTION
by Michael Calvert

Previous contributors have looked at reasons for reflection, subjects to reflect on and how to reflect; what is also needed is a framework in which the process of change and development can take place. Action research, often referred to as classroom-based research, provides such a framework.

Action research offers a flexible approach to reflection and change by incorporating research techniques in an examination of what is taking place in the classroom. This research has been developed in a variety of ways, but the cycle of activity can be shown as follows:

Figure 6

The action research cycle

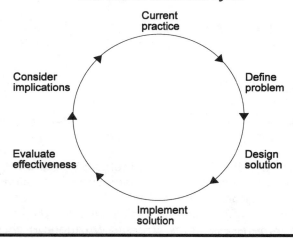

The steps involve teachers:

- looking at an area of teaching and identifying an area they want to, need to and feel able to change;
- defining a clear goal which can be achieved within a relatively short period of time;
- setting out a plan of work and a realistic timetable;
- finding ways of recording what is happening;
- analysing the findings and evaluating successes and failures;
- hypothesising on reasons for success and extending the ideas as they think fit to other classes and situations.

Figure 7 shows both theoretical and practical steps.

The examples quoted in this contribution are taken from the case studies[1] from a project based at the University of York and led by Michael Buckby. Over 80 teachers from 25 LEAs took part in the scheme which spanned nine months and which resulted in the publication of a handbook and video[2] designed to help individuals, departments or LEAs to undertake action research.

Figure 7

Flowchart for cycle of tasks

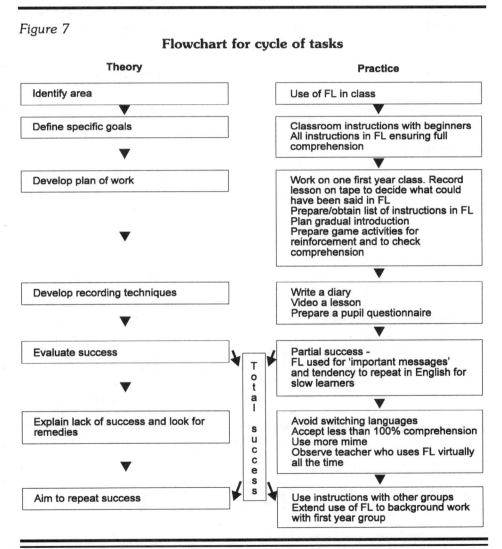

Theory	Practice
Identify area	Use of FL in class
Define specific goals	Classroom instructions with beginners All instructions in FL ensuring full comprehension
Develop plan of work	Work on one first year class. Record lesson on tape to decide what could have been said in FL Prepare/obtain list of instructions in FL Plan gradual introduction Prepare game activities for reinforcement and to check comprehension
Develop recording techniques	Write a diary Video a lesson Prepare a pupil questionnaire
Evaluate success	Partial success - FL used for 'important messages' and tendency to repeat in English for slow learners
Explain lack of success and look for remedies	Avoid switching languages Accept less than 100% comprehension Use more mime Observe teacher who uses FL virtually all the time
Aim to repeat success	Use instructions with other groups Extend use of FL to background work with first year group

Total success

1   The writer would like to thank sincerely the participants who submitted case studies and whose work enriched both the handbook and this and other articles.
2   The handbook and video are published by the University of York and are available from the Language Teaching Centre, University of York.

Getting started

The teacher working on action research may be helped by deciding on a precise focus. We are all aware of our strengths and weakness but it can be demanding to have to narrow down our objectives and set realistic goals for improvement. This proved to be very difficult for some. 'Motivating a low-ability class', for example, proved to be too wide a focus for one teacher. The need to address simultaneously all aspects of teaching from planning to assessment was out of the question and the topic was abandoned early on. The teacher recognised that gathering meaningful data and measuring the results would have been impossible.

Once the focus had been selected, the next task is to devise a plan. One teacher wrote:

> *'I deliberately chose two groups which would, I thought, respond positively to the challenge. Perhaps this was cowardice on my part.'*

On the contrary, this seems eminently sensible. The goals must be realistic and achievable in a short space of time. As shown in Figure 2 (page 38), it is possible to identify one group or even one period a week so as not to overburden oneself. Timing, too, is crucial. One participant wrote:

> *'The project was short-lived. I started in a fit of enthusiasm just before the Easter break, and then found that any momentum that we had created had disappeared when we returned.'*

The importance of morale should not be underestimated. The pressure of teaching with 'training days, and an exchange to France, plus county courses and two days out when the school was closed during the recent storm due to power failure - to mention but a few' means that anticipating problems, calling on support and looking for early success are vital. Teachers were encouraged to work in groups for mutual support, and one participant commented that the meetings were *'most beneficial in the sharing of concepts and ideas, and the testing and developing of topics in a practical working environment'*.

'Give me feedback but be gentle to me'

Having decided on a focus and drawn up a plan of action, the next step is to gather data on what is happening in the classroom and any changes which are being implemented. The taxonomy of techniques is extensive (c.f. Hopkins, 1985) and only some can be covered here.

A popular means of gathering data was to use a sympathetic observer. The above quotation reveals the vulnerability of the class teacher who may well be insecure and unaccustomed to having visitors in the lesson.

In action research, the observer is briefed as to the precise focus and, rather than sitting in judgement as is often the case with observers, is merely an instrument of the other's improvement. The power relationship is reversed - the teacher is in charge, **not** the observer.

Other common techniques were audio and video recording, questionnaires and teacher and pupil diaries. The choice of technique is determined by the focus and the researcher's aim to find out as much information as possible to inform their practice. The results of most techniques were predictable. Interestingly, what impressed participants most was the value of involving pupils in the process of research and change. One stated:

> *'They (the pupils) responded well to knowing that they were part of a study and, I feel, commented fairly freely and honestly at the end both formally in the questionnaire and informally in conversation. The experience of participating in the work seems in itself to have increased their confidence and encouraged involvement.'*

Indeed, pupils proved to be very frank. The following statements were made by one class talking about flexible learning:

> *'You're knackered at the end of the lesson if you've worked hard enough.'*

> *'You're in charge.'*

> *'You don't always need the teacher.'*

> *'If you cheat, you cheat yourself.'*

This degree of honesty was reflected in a number of cases and helped encourage other teachers to involve the pupils in the process.

Examining the evidence

It must be acknowledged that this area was not the most successful aspect of the project. Insufficient time, teachers running out of steam at the end of a term/year, a satisfaction with the outcomes to date, a lack of confidence in being able to apply research methodology could all account for this. One of the teachers confessed to relying on *'Teacher-gut-reaction-as-remembered-well-after-the-event-while-typing-up-the-report'*. As Hopkins (1985, p43) makes clear:

> *It is no excuse at all to claim that rigour is unnecessary because the research is practitioner-oriented, small-scale, or used solely to improve individual practice. If a change in teaching strategy is to be made, then that decision needs to be based on reliable data.*

The gains would, undoubtedly, have been greater had there been more perseverance and self-belief on the part of the participants but, even so, the results were very promising.

Outcomes

Such a rigorous approach to reflection and a commitment to personal and professional development is demanding and teachers need to be convinced of its worth. Evidence from the project showed that teachers:

• were more aware of the need for this type of 'on-going' training rather than relying on 'one-off' courses;

• had gained the confidence and willingness to share ideas and take more responsibility for their training;

• had identified other related areas of their teaching which needed to be improved.

Conclusions

Systematic reflection requires commitment and discipline. To claim that action research is easy would be misleading. Yet the benefits of the approach have long been recognised. Whether it be an individual, departmental or LEA initiative, whether it be to implement or monitor change, it is flexible enough to accommodate reflection at the deepest level.

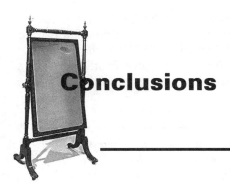

Conclusions

Although one principal theme to emerge from this book has been that of teachers taking personal responsibility for their professional development in an open-minded way - and many teachers of course show themselves to be capable of fully independent reflection - Chapter 5 has also considered the potential value of various levels of support in getting started. The hard-pressed nature of the contemporary teacher's job has been acknowledged; so, too, the potential morale problems of the individual teacher faced with a barrage of directed change. These factors make very understandable the pleasure of sharing concerns with and working alongside others. Nevertheless, for many, this social support which helps initiate and sustain reflection soon becomes secondary to the practical goals of their reflection. Secondary, that is, to the cycles of e.g. review, experiment and re-evaluation which Michael Calvert describes above and which constitute the essence of reflective practice.

Networking

At the same time, if the maximum benefit is to be derived from reflective practice in particular schools and classrooms, there may be a need for some activity beyond the level of the individual. To begin with, of course, insights can usefully be shared. If more generally known, they can be acted upon and also form starting-points for other reflective practitioners in their turn. This is where the concept of the 'teacher-researcher network' comes into its own. However, networks are not mere sharing devices for the results of work which is already complete. There are other equally effective means whereby findings can be more widely disseminated. The special role and value of networks lies in providing a framework of ideas as well as a bank of encouragement, experience and skills which can help and encourage newcomers as well as support those whose work is in progress.

The point has been well put by Bridget Somekh; for instance, in her address to the 1989 conference of one of the most flourishing and best-supported networks, the Collaborative Action Research Network (CARN) at the Centre for Applied Research in Education, based in the University of East Anglia. She spoke then of sharing '*a belief that the research process is fundamentally important to development and change*'. She continued:

> '*We may not call the work we do action research... the name is unimportant. We may call it 'paired observation', 'classroom inquiry', 'school-centred INSET', 'self-evaluation', 'teacher research', or simply 'teaching'. What unites us is the belief that reflection on our own practice is the key to professional development and the continuing development of the curriculum.*'

The words of her final sentence are carefully chosen, deliberately linking the professional development of the individual with the general development of classroom curricular practice. They thus carry several important implications, for instance:

- that a powerful basis for classroom change is evolutionary, teacher-owned and dependent upon evaluation and experiment;

- that such a change benefits profoundly from teacher participation in decisions about its purpose and the form it should take, not just the practicalities of carrying it out;

- that the local expertise vested in teachers can underpin relevant investigations which, while embracing the future professional development of the individual teacher, can also go on to include activity well worthy of the term 'research' in the curriculum field.

Indeed, a collaborative action research framework can lend a greater degree of credibility to the interpretation of evidence than a lone classroom-visiting researcher necessarily achieves, however skilled or experienced that 'outside' researcher may be.

For the purposes of the present chapter, the point is that various kinds of collaborative reflection can make the start of a project easier as well as the later phases more productive. Initial discussion with a colleague may not only be a source of courage for making a start; it can also help the necessary trust to develop which often pays dividends at later stages when potentially awkward questions about each other's teaching may have to be faced. If such a framework of trust is developed, those questions can be asked and considered in dialogue and be all the better thought-through in that way.

To summarise: although reflective practice is ultimately the responsibility of the individual teacher as a true professional, some form of social or intellectual support may be invaluable in helping individuals to make the transition into it. Support can take less formal as well as more formal shape; and it can underpin quality of outcome as well as motivation.

We hope that previous chapters, as well as this one, will have offered an encouraging picture of what reflective practice can mean for teachers of modern foreign languages, particularly at this time. We also hope that the benefits and enthusiasm made evident by our contributors will provide a resource of ideas and advice for others to build on.

Suggested further reading

Clear accounts of, as well as arguments in favour of, reflective practice are contained in this first group of titles.

Kyriacou C, *Essential teaching skills* (Simon and Schuster, 1991)

Richards J and D Nunan (eds), *Second language teacher education* (Cambridge University Press, 1990)

Russell T and H Munby (eds), *Teachers and teaching: from classroom to reflection* (Falmer Press, 1992)

Smyth J, *Teachers as collaborative learners* (Open University Press, 1991)

Kyriacou includes reflective skills among those which he sees as the 'essential' requirement of the professional teacher. Russell and Munby, as well as Smyth, chart a similar path in general terms, while Richards and Nunan offer a more specific focus on the needs of language teachers. They argue that the necessary foundations need to be laid within initial training and supported thereafter.

Useful advice on ways in which to gather and use evidence, with particular reference to languages classrooms, is given by:

Allwright R, *Observation in the language classroom* (Longman, 1988)

Allwright R and K Bailey, *Focus on the language classroom* (Cambridge University Press, 1991)

Brumfit C J and R Mitchell (eds), *Research in the language classroom* (Modern English Publications in association with the British Council, 1990)

Johnstone R, *Communicative interaction: a guide for language teachers* (CILT, 1989)

Peck A, *Language teachers at work* (Prentice Hall, 1988)

While Peck's study presents an interesting picture of customary practice through observation of a range of language classrooms, his own methods of investigation and the ways in which he displays evidence offer an illustration to put alongside the advice about topics and methods to be found in the other volumes. Johnstone's account, e.g. of teachers who appear 'enabling', also provides some excellent starting points.

Advice on classroom inquiry of a more general kind is given by:

Edwards A and D Westgate, *Investigating classroom talk* (Falmer Press, 1987)

Hopkins D, *A teacher's guide to classroom research* (Oxford University Press, 1985)

The assumptions and practices of various traditions of classroom research in which language-data are used form the framework of the first of these books, though extensive advice on practical matters such as recording and transcription is also given - e.g. Chapter 3. Hopkins was one of the first to write directly to a teacher/researcher audience and this book also contains plenty of sound practical advice adaptable to MFL classrooms.

References

Alexander D, D Muir and D Chant, 'Interrogating stories: how teachers think they learned to teach', *Teaching and teacher education*, 8, 1; 59-68 (1992)

Allwright R, 'Prescription and description in the training of language teachers', Association Internationale de Linguistique Appliquée: 3rd congress (Copenhagen); *Proceedings*, Vol 3, Heidelberg (Julius Gross Verlag, 1972)

Allwright R, *Observation in the language classroom* (Longman, 1988)

Allwright R and K Bailey, *Focus on the language classroom* (Cambridge University Press, 1991)

Bailey K, 'The use of diary studies in teacher education programmes' in Richards J and D Nunan (eds) *Second language teacher education* (Cambridge University Press, 1990)

Brumfit C J and R Mitchell (eds), *Research in the language classroom* (Modern English Publications in association with the British Council, 1990)

Calderhead J, 'Reflective teaching and teacher education', *Teaching and teacher education*, 5, 1; 43-51 (1989)

Calderhead J and P Gates (eds), *Conceptualising reflection in teacher development*, (Falmer Press, 1993)

Calderhead J and M Robson, 'Images of teaching: student teachers' early conceptions of classroom practice', *Teaching and teacher education*, 7, 1; 1-8 (1991)

DES/Welsh Office, *Modern foreign languages for ages 11 to 16 - proposals of the Secretary of State for Education and Science and the Secretary of State for Wales* (HMSO, 1990)

Dewey J, *How we think* (Heath and Co, 1933)

Edwards A and D Westgate, *Investigating classroom talk* (Falmer Press, 1987)

Halliwell S and B Jones, *On target: teaching in the target language* (Pathfinder 5) (CILT, 1991)

Handal G and P Lauvas, *Promoting reflective teaching: supervision in action* (Open University Press, 1987)

Her Majesty's Inspectorate of Schools (HMI), *Quality in schools: the initial training of teachers* (HMSO, 1987)

Her Majesty's Inspectorate of Schools (HMI), *The new teacher in school* (HMSO, 1988)

Hopkins D, *A teacher's guide to classroom research* (Oxford University Press, 1985)

Hundleby S and F Breet, 'Using methodology notebooks on in-service teacher training courses', *English Language Teaching Journal*, 41, 2 (1988)

Johnstone R, *Communicative interaction: a guide for language teachers* (CILT, 1989)

Korthagen F A J, 'The influence of learning orientations on the development of reflective teaching' in Calderhead J (ed), *Teacher's professional learning* (Falmer Press, 1988)

Kyriacou C, *Essential teaching skills* (Simon and Schuster, 1991)

Levin L, *Comparative studies in foreign language teaching: the GUME project* (Alqvist and Wiskell, 1972)

Livingstone C and H Borko, 'Expert-novice differences in teaching: a cognitive analysis and implications for teacher education', *Journal of Teacher Education*, July-August; 36-42 (1989)

Long M H, 'Inside the black box: methodological issues in classroom research on language learning', *Language Learning*, 30, 1; 1-42 (1980)

Lowe T, 'An experiment in role reversal: teachers as language learners', *English Language Teaching Journal*, 41, 2; 89-96 (1987)

Mitchell R, B Parkinson and R Johnstone, *The foreign language classroom: an observational study* (University of Stirling, Department of Education, 1981)

National Curriculum Council, *Modern foreign languages non-statutory guidance* (NCC, 1992)

Nunan D, *Understanding language classrooms: a guide for teacher initiated action* (Prentice Hall, 1989)

Palmer C, 'Diary studies for self-assessment and INSET programme evaluation', *European Journal of Teacher Education*, 15, 3 (1992)

Palmer G, 'The practical feasibility of diary studies for INSET', *European Journal of Teacher Education*, 15, 3 (1992)

Peck A, *Language teachers at work* (Prentice Hall, 1988)

Peck A, 'Teacher talk and pupil talk: a case study approach in effective foreign language teaching', *Language Learning Journal*, 2; 5-10 (1990)

Phillips D (ed), *Languages in schools: from complacency to conviction* (CILT, 1988)

Pollard A and S Tann, *Reflective teaching in the primary school* (Cassell, 1987)

Richards J and D Nunan (eds), *Second language teacher education* (Cambridge University Press, 1990)

Russell T and H Munby (eds), *Teachers and teaching: from classroom to reflection* (Falmer Press, 1992)

Scherer G A C and M Wertheimer, *A psycho-linguistic experiment in foreign language teaching* (McGraw-Hill, 1964)

Schön D, *The reflective practitioner: how professionals think in action* (Basic Books, 1983)

Schumann F, 'Diary of a language learner: a further analysis', in Scarcella R and S Krashen (eds), *Research in second language acquisition: selected papers of the Los Angles Second Language Acquisition Research Forum* (Newbury House, 1980)

Smith R, *The effective school* (Vol 2: Classroom techniques and management) (Framework Press, 1990)

Smyth J, *Teachers as collaborative learners* (Open University Press, 1991)

Somekh B, 'Opening the discourse', paper presented in the opening of the CARN International Conference, September 1989 (University of East Anglia, 1989)

Stern H H, *Fundamental concepts of language teaching* (Oxford University Press, 1983)

Tabachnik B R and K M Zeichner (eds), *Practices and issues in inquiry oriented teacher education* (Falmer Press, 1991)

Thornbury S, 'Watching the whites of their eyes: the use of teaching practice logs', *English Language Teaching Journal*, 45, 2; 140-6 (1991)

Westgate D, 'Contrasting realities in the foreign language classroom', *Language Learning Journal*, 1; 10-15 (1990)

Westgate D, J Batey, J Brownlee and M Butler, 'Some characteristics of interaction in foreign language classrooms', *British Educational Research Journal*, 11, 3; 271-81 (1985)

Westgate D, J Batey and J Brownlee, 'Collaborative action research: professional development in a cold climate', *British Journal of In-Service Education*, 16, 3; 167-72 (1990)

Winitzky N, 'Structures and process in thinking about classroom managment: an exploratory study of prospective teachers', *Teaching and Teacher Education*, 8, 1; 1-4 (1992)

The contributors

John Batey is Head of Department at Ridley High School, a 13 to 18 comprehensive, at Blyth in Northumberland. He has taught French and German in that post for 18 years, and previously at other schools in the North-East. He has been involved for over a decade, with colleagues and with David Westgate, in collaborative action research on various aspects of modern languages classrooms. He has also been a part-time Visiting Lecturer in the School of Education at the University of Newcastle-upon-Tyne.

Michael Calvert, formerly head of a comprehensive school modern languages department in Hertfordshire, is now a Lecturer in Education at the University of Sheffield, with particular concern for the initial training of language teachers. He has also lectured at the University of York, where (with Michael Buckby) he published *Towards the National Curriculum: personal and professional development; increasing autonomy*, a handbook and video for modern languages teachers embarking on action research.

Eryl Griffiths is now Director of Studies at the Cambridge Eurocentre where she has worked, woman and girl, for the last twenty years. Her other professional interests are the IATEFL Research Special Interest Group of which she is Co-ordinator, the English Language Teaching Management SIG, the Cambridge Directors of Studies Association and the Cambridge English Language Teachers Association (CELTA). She is also on the IATEFL Committee and a member of the Society for Effective and Affective Learning and Women in TEFL.

Professor Richard Johnstone is Head of the Department of Education, University of Stirling, and Director of the Scottish Centre for Information on Language Teaching and Research (Scottish CILT). He has directed many research projects for SOED on the teaching and learning of foreign or second languages, and has written several books on the subject. He is currently responsible for the evaluation of national pilot projects in modern languages in Scottish primary schools and for an EC-funded survey on teacher training for languages across all EU member states.

Diana Kent is responsible for the initial training courses for secondary teachers of foreign languages in the Education Department of Stirling University. She is qualified in Spanish, French and German and has experience of teaching a wide range of secondary schools both here and abroad, with research interests in oral communication and assessment.

Christine Korczak is Division Manager, Languages, and Senior Lecturer, at Hopwood Hall College, Middleton, Manchester, where she currently teaches German from beginners to 'A' level. She has previously taught German, French and Spanish in schools in Rochdale and Norfolk. Her research interest has covered classes in all these languages and Urdu, with a concern for the use of the target language as a teaching medium.

Chris Kyriacou is a Senior Lecturer in Educational Psychology at the Department of Educational Studies of the University of York. His first degree is in Psychology, from the University of Reading. He trained to teach mathematics at Goldsmiths' College, London, and taught in a London comprehensive school before going to a PhD at the University of Cambridge on the topic of teacher stress. He has published widely in the area of effective teaching, including a recent book entitled *Essential teaching skills* (1991).

Gill and Chris Palmer both work at Poznan, in Poland: Chris as a regional teacher-trainer with the British Council PACE Project, and Gill as a Senior Lecturer in methodology and applied linguistics at Adam Mickiewicz University. They have previously been involved in language teaching and teacher training in France, Spain, Italy, Portugal, Brazil and, more recently, at the University of York. Their current interests include literature in ELT, classroom innovation and action research.

Antony Peck is Senior Lecturer in the Language Teaching Centre at the University of York. After teaching at a grammar school in Shrewsbury, he joined the Nuffield Foreign Languages Project in York, where he led the team responsible for *Vorwärts*. From 1973 to 1986 he was Director of the Language Materials Development Unit. He is now in charge of the PGCE for linguists at York, where his research is in the field of the description and analysis of language teaching.

Jacky Ramage is a graduate of Glasgow University. She took her PGCE at Didsbury College, Manchester, and taught for three years in a Salford comprehensive. The lure of a Scale 2 (Second in Department) then took her to a Middlesborough comprehensive for three years. In 1985, she was appointed Head of Languages at De Brus School, a small rural comprehensive at Skelton, Cleveland, where she teaches French and German.

Emma Taylor studied modern languages at the University of Hull and took her degree in German and French. As part of her degree course, she lived for a year in Vienna where she taught English at the Handelsakademie. She completed her PGCE course at the Language Teaching Centre at York University in 1993 and now lives in the North-East of England.

Margaret Wells is Head of Department at Hirst High School, a 13 to 18 comprehensive, at Ashington, Northumberland. She has been teaching French and German in that post for 14 years, having previously taught in grammar schools and three other comprehensives in the North-East. During this time she has taken an MA in German and MEd, both at the University of Newcastle-upon-Tyne, and is currently registered there for PhD research in education.

David Westgate is a Senior Lecturer in Education at the School of Education of the University of Newcastle-upon-Tyne, where he is involved in initial training of modern languages teachers as well as in in-service courses in language in education. Before that he taught French and German in Croydon and was Head of the French Department at the Froebel Institute, Roehampton. His research has included aspects of classroom talk (in English) at both primary and secondary phases; he has, however, particularly emphasised collaborative action research with teachers in modern languages classrooms.